VANESSA VENNING   MARIANNE PERKOVIC

pivotal
CAREER
MOMENTS

HOW *CONFIDENCE* CAN IMPACT CAREER SUCCESS AND WHAT TO DO ABOUT IT

Acknowledgements

Together, we would like to express our heartfelt gratitude to all those who supported and inspired us through this journey – to the many friends, colleagues and people we are yet to meet, who contributed their time in completing our survey, and to the professional women we interviewed, who openly shared their personal stories and lived experience of their careers. It was these experiences that shaped the direction of this book.

Thank you to our book coach, Kath Walters, and the team at Publish Central, Michael Hanrahan, Charlotte Duff and Anna Clemann.

Special thanks to our friend Krista Fraser, who read our first draft and whose constructive feedback enriched this book. Also thanks to Peggy Vosloo, whose visual designs brought the Think Beyond model to life, and Andrew Inwood and Alison Sweet from Core Data, who helped analyse our survey results.

Lastly, we thank you, our reader, whose engagement with these pages completes the circle of our creation.

Thanks, from Marianne

I would like to thank my incredible family for their unconditional love and support in every aspect of my life, both professionally and personally. My gratitude knows no bounds for the lessons you've taught me. First and foremost, thanks to my ultimate role models – my mum and dad, they are my guiding lights. My loving and supportive husband, Chris, has been my pillar of strength. My daughters, Annabell and Alanna, continually inspire me to be a better human. Thanks to my mother-in-law, Diane, and the memory of my late father-in-law, Mike, for their encouragement. My sister, Lilly, brother-in-law, Joe, brother, Adrian, and sister-in-law, Marieka, and my nephews and nieces, Anthony, Michael, Alexander, Gabriella, Scarlett and Nicholas, and the memory of my late brother-in-law, Matt – thank you for being the best partners in life, keeping it fun and grounding. Special mention also to my dear friends who are family – Krista, Ben and Nat, Kharen and Garry, and Tanja and Andy.

To all the amazing people over the decades who I have worked with, alongside or worked directly for me – it's been a privilege and I've cherished every moment of learning from each one of you. Special thanks to Linda, Helen, Anne, Maria, Penni, Lex, Ian, Leif, Susan and Tanya. I couldn't have asked for better people in facing the challenges and opportunities, all while striving to create a more enjoyable, diverse and inclusive environment.

Thanks, from Vanessa

Thank you to my husband, Neal, for your love, support and patience enabling me to focus on this book, and to my children, Matthew, Ashley and Olivia, whom I love and adore. I am so proud of the young adults you have become. Go forward with courage and confidence!

To my wonderful mum and dad, I'll be forever grateful for the loving upbringing and opportunities you've given my brother Peter and me. My cousin Carol joined me in Sydney decades ago and has been my family rock and supporter. My 'Sister' Karen and husband Jim, we have travelled far and wide together and you've been there for me no matter what. I'm forever grateful to have you in my life.

To the special friends who became my family away from home over 30 years ago, known affectionately as 'the Goddesses', your friendship, wisdom, unconditional love and support have enriched my life forever. Thank you to my friend and wellbeing buddy "Running Robyn" for regularly starting our days together, and together with the wonderful friends and colleagues who have been my cheer squad and sounding board, your continued enthusiasm inspires me to be a better person.

To the executive women and men I have supported through coaching – walking beside you as part of your career journey has been a privilege. I continue to learn from you every day. Thank you!

In memory of my colleague Conor O'Malley. His encouragement and generosity inspired me to follow in his footsteps on this journey to authorship. May he rest in peace.

NATIONAL LIBRARY OF AUSTRALIA

A catalogue entry for this book is available from the National Library of Australia.

ISBN: 978-1-922764-59-1

Printed in Australia
Book production and text design by Publish Central
Cover design by Pipeline Design

The paper this book is printed on is certified as environmentally friendly.

Contents

Introduction

We have each worked in an array of executive roles and industries for over three decades (and counting!). And what we started to notice over this time was a strange and common experience occurring for successful senior executives – and it was most prominent in women. Women who had previously been rock solid in their confidence found themselves at breaking point in their career. Corporate or personal pressures built up to a point that felt unbearable. At a time in their lives when you would expect their confidence to be at a peak, it plummeted to all-time lows. These women felt crippled by this experience and struggled to navigate through.

This was devastating for us to witness, and we both wanted to do something about it. However, we first needed to understand what was happening. We immersed ourselves in studying this topic and expanded our understanding beyond the existing articles and books by conducting our own research. As we set out to research the issue of women's confidence and its potential to unravel, we started to recognise a particular moment when everything appeared to become too much. And we came to call these moments *pivotal career moments* (PCMs), a term we'd seen mentioned that seemed to capture the experience. When women were faced with a PCM at a senior level, their confidence was rocked, despite all their experience and skills. We likened the resulting plummet in confidence – and the growing sense of stress and anxiety – to a snowball gathering momentum down a mountain. And this reduction in confidence affected the health and wellbeing, relationships and careers of these women.

Why we wrote this book

We have not only witnessed these PCMs, but also gained our own unique lived experience of them, and we will share some of these moments throughout the book. We have both experienced the drop in confidence that can follow a PCM. We know what this moment – and the lead-up to it – feels like, and how the hit to your confidence and increased anxiety and stress can all build up to a huge snowball that starts to tumble.

Over two decades of executive and board experience in the banking and financial services sector, Marianne observed few women in senior and board roles. Often, she was the only female, and still is to this day. As she progressed through the ranks, many women she worked alongside with left the corporate world, often due to the inflexibility of the corporate world to cater for their caring responsibilities – either after having children or to look after aged parents (or both). But she realised having to take up a caregiver role wasn't the only factor. Over her career, she also began to observe women have PCMs and later personally experienced a PCM herself – and felt the impact of this on her confidence. She also noticed this hit to confidence seemed to be far greater for women than for men, and that men appeared to bounce back quicker than women. This made her curious to learn more to understand this issue better and share the learnings to support others. Her own PCM made Marianne rethink her motivations for her next career step and she decided to transition to a portfolio career. A portfolio career is a career path where individuals pursue diverse roles simultaneously, tailored to their skills, strengths and interests, rather than having a traditional job with a single employer. For Marianne, this path has created a more flexible and varied work life that has in turn created greater autonomy and creativity, and built a unique professional identity.

Vanessa started her career as a registered nurse but also landed in the spotlight as a professional performer, having secured a recording contract after winning Bert Newton's *New Faces* when she was in her teens. She later performed and presented on television, and secured a contract with the Seven Network to co-host and sing for major television events as well as presenting weather for the evening news. Driven to escape some of the sexism within the entertainment industry, Vanessa went back to university to study business and human resources, and moved into an executive career across various sectors, including technology, professional services, the travel industry, broadcast media, retail, luxury brands and medical devices.

No-one would have ever suspected that Vanessa was anything but supremely confident. Behind the scenes, however, she sometimes struggled with the lack of support for young female executives in her often pioneering roles. Vanessa hit a moment that she now knows to be a PCM – brought about by three children under three and a high-pressure role. She suffered a horrible drop in confidence, and experienced firsthand the disconnect that can arise between seeming outwardly confident and the stress and anxiety that is really going on underneath. Eventually realising it was time for a change, Vanessa transitioned to become an executive coach working with senior leaders across global businesses. Coaching numerous talented senior executives, Vanessa noticed an imbalance. More women seemed to be struggling with this confidence issue, and the negative impact on them seemed to be greater. This ignited Vanessa's obsession with helping women who experienced PCMs.

Our paths crossed in 2017, when we both had daughters at the same school; however, it wasn't until 2019, on a plane trip to Singapore to support our daughters who were part of the school band, that we discovered we were both on the same mission – to help executive women overcome what we observed as a lack of confidence and stress snowball during their PCMs. We both had the goal to write a book to help others. We decided to support each other and join forces to write this book, based on our lived, professional and observed experience.

We supplemented what we knew with our own research into this topic. This included online surveys and virtual or face-to-face interviews with 123 executives. These took place over 2020–21. These executives were Australian-based leaders in senior roles – including C-suite (CEOs, CFOs and CIOs), managing directors, non-executive directors and chairs – in industries covering banking and finance, technology, media, entertainment, wealth management, resources, health and disability support. These executives also worked across a range of businesses, from large ASX-listed corporates, government, not-for-profit and for-purpose organisations, to private business, associations, start-ups and scale-up businesses. Overwhelmingly, our research found:

- Both men and women believe men are more confident than women. Of the women we surveyed, 89 per cent believed men were more confident than women, while 67 per cent of men shared this view.
- Lack of confidence has hindered the career progression of half of all the women we surveyed, and almost all of them have suffered from imposter syndrome.
- The three key contributors to the lack of confidence snowball are psychologically unsafe corporate environments, not acknowledging or prioritising health and wellbeing, and the absence of a supportive crew.
- PCMs can happen to everyone, and can play a massive role in confidence and the ability to achieve success.

- A bad experience in a PCM can cripple confidence and lead to feelings of self-doubt and inadequacy – and if you don't navigate through these moments, you may find yourself facing a career avalanche.
- You can navigate through your PCM and continue your career successfully.

We've included extracts from our interviews to expand on our ideas and provide real-life examples throughout the book. The research and stories in our book are real stories shared by real people who we have interviewed; due to privacy protocols, we have changed our interviewee names but not their role descriptions.

We did this additional research because we take this issue seriously, and we've seen the severe consequences on executive women's lives and careers – caused by not only PCMs but also the way women deal with these moments in their aftermath. We also wanted to take all our learnings and give executives tools to help them navigate through their PCM. The main tool is our model which we named the Think Beyond model.

The Think Beyond model

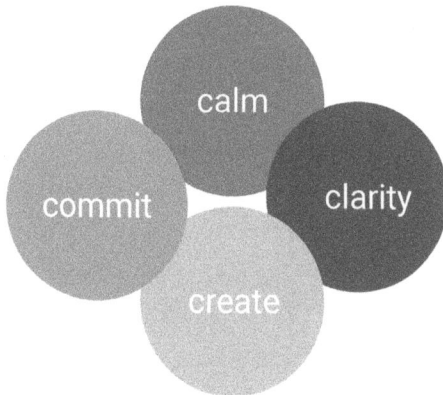

Who this book is for

Both males and females in senior roles have experienced confidence dips throughout their career. We acknowledge that not all men have unshakeable confidence. What we have noticed from our professional and personal experiences, and what was subsequently verified in our research, is that senior executive women often experience a greater struggle with a snowballing decline of confidence during a PCM. (In this book, we use the term 'executive' to describe senior roles that can be either executive or non-executive – for example, a board director.) We have written this book for executive women who have experienced the feelings of stress and anxiety associated with a PCM, and for executives who, despite career success to date, may currently be struggling to find their way through a confidence snowball or even a career avalanche. We've also written this to help executive women who haven't yet experienced a PCM to be forewarned and prepared.

We aim to provide guidance to female executives who want evidence-based strategies to implement for themselves or to assist others as they navigate their PCM. While focusing on executive women, we believe men and women alike can benefit from the introspective approach and insights to be gained from this book. We encourage executive men to read this book to gain an understanding of the lived experiences of executive women. This book draws on the experiences of the women in the industries we have exposure to, and we continue to find the themes are agnostic to any specific industry.

When faced with a PCM, most women can feel alone and don't want to share what can feel like a very personal experience. We hope this book helps you understand that you are not alone. Many other executives feel the same. We've outlined stories from incredibly successful and amazing executive women, and what you will learn is even these women had their confidence rocked; however, they all bounced back, and you will learn how. After reading this book, you'll also be better able to bounce back when experiencing a PCM.

Perhaps you're reading this book and know you are experiencing a PCM, or perhaps deep down you know that you are not completely happy. One of the reasons why you may be feeling this way is that you may not know that it's a PCM that is contributing to those feelings. The information and tools provided here can help you navigate through that moment more quickly. If you're stuck in the recent aftermath of a PCM, this book can help you understand your situation and provide some key learnings. And if you haven't yet gone through a PCM, but have seen the warning signs, this book can help ensure you're doing things now to prepare better for that moment.

How to use this book

This book gives you the tools to navigate a PCM, bounce back quicker and get your wellbeing in balance so you can get back on track for a successful career.

In part I, we do a deep dive into the importance of confidence and how it affects your career potential. We help you identify and anticipate your PCM and understand the relationship this has with your confidence (or lack of). In part II, we outline the top three areas, based on our research, that contribute to the lack of confidence snowball – psychologically unsafe working environments, not prioritising health and wellbeing, and the absence of a supportive crew. And in part III, we take you through our Think Beyond model for more effectively dealing with, and learning from, a PCM. This model focuses on four key areas – calm, clarity, create and commit – to help you step outside the stress and anxiety of a PCM and literally think beyond it. Calm is about awareness, and shifting the focus to managing stress to enable optimal thinking. This consciousness enables clarity to be rebuilt around identity, reconnecting with passion, purpose, values and signature strengths. This is the necessary foundation to identify options and creatively come up with a new plan for working through your PCM. From there, you can commit to the goals required to execute successfully.

We couldn't end our book without putting this into a macro perspective, and in the final chapter we have included key facts and figures to help you understand your confidence crisis in the context of some of the systematic issues working against women.

Throughout chapters 1 to 10, we've also included 'Reflection point' breakout boxes. Here we provide exercises and prompts to help you apply the information to your specific experience and start taking action. We suggest you write your responses, reflections, insights and plans in a journal – either a physical book or electronically (whichever method suits you). Whatever its format, be sure to keep and treasure this journal as your personal journey of thoughts and reflection.

We want to reassure you that you will get through this. In this book, we provide you with the tools and knowledge to do so, based on our years of experience, the research we've undertaken with highly successful executive women and their stories of how they have navigated this journey to think beyond.

Instead of derailing your career, you can use this book to recognise when you are stuck and your confidence is falling. You will find you are not alone, and that this is an experience also shared by some of the most senior executives in the world. Read on for a breakthrough in clarity to think beyond.

PART I

Confidence, pivotal career moments and career stages

1

Confidence and its impact on your career potential

Luck is what happens when preparation meets opportunity.
Lucius Annaeus Seneca (Roman stoic philosopher)

Our lived experience and research shows that executives describe what it means to be confident in different ways, and how they manage their confidence has different impacts on their career success. This is why the topic of confidence is so fascinating – and why so many people are trying to understand it more clearly. Thousands of books, blogs, TED Talks and articles are available about it – which can also make the topic confusing and at times overwhelming. What is most important is your understanding of what confidence means to you, your own relationship with confidence and how it can impact your own career success.

According to the Cambridge Dictionary, the word confidence comes from the Latin *confedio*, which means having full trust. Confidence (based on *certainty*) is defined as 'the quality of being certain in your abilities or of having trust in people, plans or the future'. The American version of the same dictionary offers a variation, defining confidence (based on *sure feeling*) as 'a feeling of having little doubt about yourself and your abilities, or a feeling of trust in someone or something'.

Before we go any further, it is important to clarify a key point. When we talk in this chapter (and throughout the book) about the importance of confidence and its influence on your career, we're not talking about the need to strive for overconfidence or trying to build an exaggerated confidence, or about measuring and judging yourself against others. The confidence we're talking about is based on its Latin roots – trusting yourself and your abilities, and trusting your own capability, judgement, intuition and gut. Confidence comes from trusting your skills and experience and intuition. Through your experiences and skills in knowing how to navigate certain situations, you will know the solutions to problems and issues, and have the confidence to use these solutions. When the path forward is not as clear, you still know how to navigate the situation, ask the right questions, or seek guidance or advice. This kind of confidence is also about accepting that vulnerability is okay, and trusting and valuing curiosity and your appetite to learn and grow.

In this chapter, we discuss how the executive women we interviewed describe confidence and what it means to them. We outline confidence perceptions, the differences between men and women and the impact on careers. We also discuss how not all, but many women are quick to label themselves – using terms such as 'imposter', for example – and how this labelling affects confidence. Finally, we look at how confidence and career success are linked, as we start to consider the effect on confidence of pivotal career moments (PCMs). Through the chapter, we explore and guide you through personal narratives and self-talk, self-branding, and creating space for confidence and vulnerability.

What executive women think confidence is

Identifying what confidence is and what it means to women is an important first step to gain clarity and perspective. As well as the dictionary definitions of confidence already provided, we found some nuances and some common themes in the ways our interviewees talked about confidence. In some ways, confidence can almost be a throwaway term, and its impact can be easily underrated. So, what are we really talking about here? Having a benchmark to start with is helpful, because it can be difficult in the heat of your PCM to recognise that your confidence and trust in yourself is being affected.

For us, the Latin root for confidence – *confedio* – is key to this discussion. Having full trust – in yourself and your capabilities and decisions – is critical for what we mean by confidence.

But this topic can still be a difficult one to tackle. We often keep our perceptions of our own confidence to ourselves. Once our confidence starts to drop, it can become a lonely journey of self-judgement. Our research enables you to gain another perspective, challenge that predisposition and explore what this topic means to other executive women. There is comfort in knowing you are not alone.

The first questions we asked our interviewees focused on describing confidence and what it meant to them, and outlining where they believed confidence came from. Even though we alerted interviewees beforehand of the questions we were going to ask to give them time to prepare, they still commented that it was a challenging task to give words to their thoughts and feelings. This is not surprising, given defining confidence is a personal topic and often a difficult one to answer succinctly. Most of our interviewees took around three minutes to explain what it meant to them. Some told us in preparation for the interview they did some of their own research, as well as asking their family, friends or colleagues to share their perspective on what confidence meant to them. The common theme that emerged was that defining confidence was quite complex. Many described it as personal to them and they qualified this in their definition.

To illustrate this issue, the following are verbatim quotes from some of the interviewees to describe what confidence meant to them:

- 'It's about consistency.'
- 'Making decisions where you back what you think, even if you're scared that that's not right.'
- 'Having confidence in your own judgement.'
- 'Thinking, *I've got this.*'
- 'Feeling you are worthwhile, doing a good job and that you value yourself.'
- 'Being able to withstand criticism.'
- 'Knowing your inner self, how you are feeling internally and how you project this to the external world.'
- 'Feeling good about yourself.'
- 'An underlying sense that you know what you are doing.'
- 'Feeling okay within myself, staying connected to my values, what I believe in and playing to my strengths.'
- 'A belief in myself and the contribution I can make. Embracing and valuing my unique differences.'
- 'Being comfortable with what I know and what I don't know.'
- 'Being comfortable to admit when I don't know something; being able to be vulnerable.'
- 'Enables me to operate at full capacity. I feel like I'm being me, being able to explain and express what I think and how I feel.'
- 'Self-belief to do what's right for you and not worry about what anybody else thinks.'
- 'Believing in yourself, your own capability, skills, knowledge and expertise; an innate sort of positivity.'

- 'Compassion and empathy, not only for others, but also for yourself. To have self-belief in place to top up your own cup first before you can give to others.'
- 'Something that is a balance between values and valuing yourself.'
- 'Feeling good within yourself both physically and mentally; an underlying state of being.'
- 'Feeling like you know what you are doing.'
- 'Trusting your judgement.'
- 'An acknowledgement of areas for growth and learning with resilience to take on criticism as an opportunity, not a threat.'

✎ Reflection point

Reading through the preceding quotes, did any resonate with you? What does confidence look like for you, and what lived experiences have helped you form that view? Think about the following questions and write down your answers in your journal:

- How do you describe confidence?
- What does it mean to you?
- Where do you think it comes from?

Confidence perceptions – the differences between the sexes

Based on our research, both men and women think women are less confident than men. Of the women we surveyed, 89 per cent believed men were more confident than women, while 67 per cent of men shared this view.

When asked what behaviours or traits men exhibit when they're confident, women often described men as 'overconfident' or 'cocky'. Throughout our careers, we've identified and witnessed these behaviours on display. Unfortunately, these are also the behaviours we see being rewarded, acknowledged and promoted. When you're working within this kind of culture, you can easily start comparing yourself against this behaviour. This becomes a quick, mostly unconscious reinforcement that you won't be perceived as confident without this behaviour.

Your thoughts will drive how you feel about confidence. Henry Ford, founder of the Ford Motor Company, in 1947 famously said, 'Whether you believe you can do a thing or not, you are right'. What he is referring to is that confidence is all about mindset and perception of behaviour – it is about your confidence in your abilities.

In our experience, men and women express confidence in different ways. Male confidence is often seen as a combination of behaviours – being vocal and loud, posturing, taking risks, strategically taking on career moves, and political manoeuvring. These behaviours have been associated with confidence. Of course, what we see isn't always what's below the surface. Marianne has worked with and Vanessa has coached many male clients where they haven't aligned with this stereotypical assessment of confidence in terms of behaviours and, as a result, assess themselves as not confident.

However, what we have seen is when women try to model these 'male' behaviours, there is a misalignment. Women who emulate men's behaviour are often labelled as overconfident, bossy or arrogant. Trying to project more confidence than you have, or display it differently from how you feel comfortable, eventually ends in behaving incongruently with your own values and beliefs, creating a state of inauthenticity. Authenticity comes from understanding what drives your own confidence, based on your own values and beliefs. Think about an iceberg as an analogy. As shown in figure 1, the behaviour on display is represented by the part of the iceberg you can see, above the water line. Our thoughts, beliefs and values, coupled with feelings and emotions, all sit below the water line but should be the basis for our behaviour. A top-heavy, behaviour-focused iceberg will quickly become unstable without a solid base below the surface.

Figure 1: The behaviour on display versus the emotions, thoughts, beliefs, feelings and values below the surface

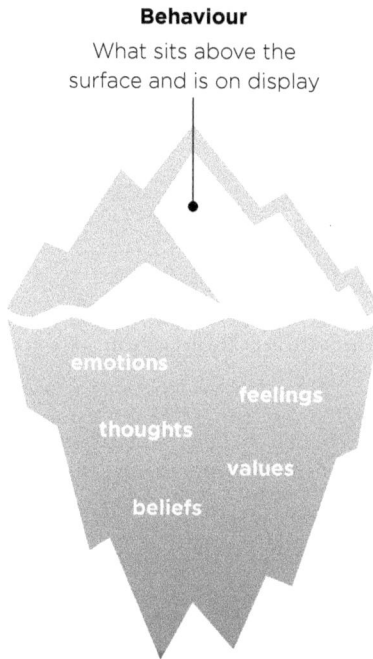

Behaviour
What sits above the
surface and is on display

emotions

feelings

thoughts

values

beliefs

So if confidence is our own personal journey in trusting our ability, how can this manifest itself in an authentic external display of behaviour? We are talking about an internal experience – how we feel and our trust in our ability – being projected. A different set of behaviours manifests with this kind of thinking. To continue the iceberg analogy, the parts people can see and the parts they can't see are much more in sync. Even though people can't see them, the thoughts, beliefs, values, feelings and emotions below the water line become foundational in driving our behaviour, which is what others see on the surface.

You may challenge us on the following broad statement, or you may already know this, but here goes. Men are not the best role models for confidence in women. What is important is to understand the differences and know how to work with them.

We asked our executive survey participants (male and female) to nominate a business leader who they thought exuded confidence. Three of the top four most commonly identified leaders were men, including Alan Joyce (former Chief Executive Officer and Managing Director Qantas Airways), Richard Branson (British billionaire, entrepreneur and founder of the Virgin Group), and Andrew Forrest (Australian businessman and former CEO of Fortescue Metals), with Jacinda Ardern (former Prime Minister of New Zealand) taking forth position. Around a third of women chose a male leader; however, the majority did choose a female business leader. After reviewing the comments provided, we saw that the women we surveyed admire female leaders who balance stereotypically female traits – for example, compassion and empathy – with strength, character and intellect. Perhaps as expected, some also cited female leaders' demeanour and poise. This demonstrates the congruency between thoughts, beliefs, values and emotions is necessary for authentic leadership.

An example of females valuing these traits was one of our interviewees Amelia, a former CEO and now non-executive director and chair for several ASX-listed organisations. She made a point when describing confidence and her own personal journey that she has never shied away from her femininity and embraced this as part of her authentic leadership. She sees this as a point of difference, adding valuable perspective and diverse thinking to the boardroom.

✐ Reflection point

Refer to your reflections about what you think confidence is and describe how you feel when you are confident. What are your thoughts? What are your beliefs and emotions around confidence? How does this relate with how you would expect to behave? Note down any differences between how you define confidence and what it means to you, and how you think you're expected to behave.

Women love labels

In our experience, women can be quick to label themselves – and we are not referring to your favourite designer label that gives you a hit of dopamine during the shopping spree here. We are referring to the internal hidden and habit-forming critical labels women place on themselves. In response to one of our survey questions on how people felt or thought when they lacked confidence, 59 per cent of survey respondents identified negative self-talk or self-criticism. Of those, 62 per cent were women and 38 per cent were men. Importantly, this kind of negative self-talk affects what is happening in our brain, and changing the tone of this narrative can have a huge impact on our confidence and resilience.

An overwhelming majority of the executive women in our research stated they have suffered from what they labelled as 'imposter syndrome'. Let's look into the definition of imposter syndrome versus what has become a label to pin on and add to our collection – as another thing that affects our perception of our own confidence. According to the Merriam-Webster dictionary, imposter syndrome is defined as 'a psychological condition that is characterised by persistent doubt concerning one's abilities or accomplishments accompanied by the fear of being exposed as a fraud, despite evidence of one's ongoing success'.

When women tell themselves they haven't reached the required standard or they don't deserve to have a seat at the table, they don't take credit for success when earned. They focus on external factors, rather than acknowledging the internal factors that contribute to success. Labels we apply – based on gender stereotypes, our upbringing, culture and values – all play a role in this syndrome.

Our interviewee Audrey is an actuary, author and non-executive director in the superannuation and wealth management industry. She spoke of the feeling of imposter syndrome when she got into university – despite doing well academically at school and getting into actuarial studies, she didn't think of herself as innately intelligent. Instead, she felt she had only gotten the results she did because she studied hard. She shared with us that she spent her first year thinking she would get 'found out'.

Every label is a thought that is creating or strengthening a neural pathway in your brain. Ongoing negative thought processes not only reinforce existing pathways and programming but can also reduce the number of positive receptors. These negative thoughts trigger the production of stress hormones, which produce feelings of nervousness, fear and anxiety – and reduce confidence. But the reverse is also true. Positive labels create neural pathways as well, and increase confidence.

Continuing on the negative pathway means the stress hormones are on overdrive and can result in chronic health issues, which we discuss further in chapter 5. This perfect but potent cocktail can lead to feelings of shame, negativity and despair. These are all perfect conditions for a confidence decline – what we've called a confidence snowball – and, if left to continue, can lead to a career avalanche.

Our research indicates negative labels, self-talk and self-criticism are the most frequent response when women are asked to think about what holds them back from their achievements.

Another example of this is our interviewee Sarika, a non-executive director and former chair of a large national association representing women. Sarika told us a story about her participation in a board development program. Despite her successful career and the merit-based approach that earnt her a place on the program, when she reviewed the credentials of the other 12 female participants, she started to question her selection. Further, when the group met, every participant revealed that they also felt like they were an imposter, and again this was despite each of them being very successful in their own right.

Our interviewee Emma is an executive in the media industry, and a journalist, presenter and author. She also shared that she has constant internal negative self-talk and questions her abilities, and that this ongoing narrative has continued to reduce her confidence. She also told us that others would never recognise this in her demeanour, because she is often described as a confident conference moderator, interviewer and presenter; however, internally her relationship with confidence is not a pleasant one and we will explore this further in chapter 3.

Imposter syndrome and other negative self-talk can become thinking habits. We explore this as we progress through this book, but let's start with a couple of small steps. Psychologist Dr Susan David talks about 'job crafting', which she describes as 'looking creatively at your work circumstances, however difficult, and finding ways to reconfigure your situation to make it more engaging and fulfilling'. Another technique is reframing – a widely used technique that helps to break the pattern – and infective nature – of negative thinking. This involves identifying a negative thinking pattern, and then countering or repositioning this with a contradictory thought. This helps you move from over-thinking and inaction to reframing the thought and taking action. Here are some examples of negative self-talk and how they can be reframed:

- 'I shouldn't have made that mistake.' *becomes* 'Everyone makes mistakes. Nobody's perfect. An error may have occurred, but it didn't change the overall outcome. What are the steps to progress from here?'

- 'I'm afraid of getting it wrong.' *becomes* 'What is the worst thing that can happen and what learning experience can I notch up along the way? What would I tell my friend if they were feeling this way?'

- 'Am I really good enough to do this job?' *becomes* 'They believe I can do the role. I was appointed via a fair and rigorous selection process.'

- 'I'm not good at office politics.' *becomes* 'I can build strong relationships. What are the steps I can take to build relationships across all stakeholders?'

- 'I don't have all the answers.' *becomes* 'It's unrealistic to know everything, so what are the important facts I need to know? I can also draw on the expertise of others.'

- 'I make poor decisions.' *becomes* 'Am I making assumptions and over-generalising? I have made many good decisions so what is another way to view this?'

- 'I can't do this anymore.' *becomes* 'I am good at this. Other people respect my ability. What is really behind me feeling this way and what steps can I take to acknowledge and address these?'

> ✏️ **Reflection point**
>
> What are your negative thinking patterns? Start to think about where this negative self-talk may be coming from.
>
> Track your thinking in your journal and identify where your thinking distortions are. Challenge yourself. What is factually correct and what isn't? How can you reframe this?

Career success and confidence are linked

Our personal experience and our research demonstrate that your career success is linked with your level of confidence. The more confidence you have, the better you feel internally and behave externally. This confident mindset enables you to make decisions that help you continue your successful career. Many factors impact confidence, and this book is not going to cover them all; however, it is important to understand that, generally, the things that are out of your control will have the greatest impact on reducing your overall confidence. The things that are likely out of your control include the environment that you're in (for example, the corporate environment), your health and wellbeing (such as unexpected sickness or illness, hormonal issues), a lack of support from your boss, and certain life events (for example, ageing parents, relationship breakdown or a new partner).

When confidence is present, you have a deeper understanding and trust in your core values, strengths, capabilities, skills, knowledge and expertise. Confidence is about accepting vulnerability – that you do not know everything and that's okay. Career success is where confidence enables you to adopt a mindset of growth and learning, ready to embrace opportunity. Career success means trust in your wisdom, solid judgement and decision-making. Confidence and career success are linked because confidence positions you in the driving seat of your career.

Just as greater confidence leads to greater career success, the opposite is also true, and tumbling confidence can lead to crippling inaction. The survey results demonstrate this. When asked the question, 'Has there ever been a time when a lack of confidence hindered you in taking on a career opportunity?', 49 per cent of the female respondents answered 'yes' (with the majority of these respondents in the 45-plus age group), compared with only 22 per cent of male respondents. This not only is a personal opportunity cost but also has an impact on business and community (which we discuss further in chapter 11).

As another example, Tenfold Australia is a multinational leadership forum providing a range of digital and in-person forums for Australian-based leaders of global companies. In October 2021, they featured an executive masterclass with Pip Marlow, the CEO of Salesforce ANZ & ASEAN, and Elizabeth Broderick, founder of the Champions of Change strategy and Australia's longest serving Sex Discrimination Commissioner. During their session, a live poll was conducted of the 128 executive attendees – with 48 per cent identifying the confidence gap in women applying for roles to be the biggest barrier to disrupting the gender divide.

Only focusing on things outside your control will reduce your confidence, which is one of the main factors that can trigger a pivotal career moment (PCM) – the topic of the next chapter. Understanding this link between confidence and career here is vital, because doing so helps you navigate these PCMs faster and more effectively. You can start to understand that it's not just happening to you – it's a process. You can learn from that process and come out of it more enriched and enlightened. In the following chapters, we continue to share the stories of our interviewees, who have reflected back on their PCM and taken away valuable learnings from their experience.

At this early stage of reading our book, we also want you to know that a PCM can happen to anyone. The feelings, thoughts and experience can be a lonely one, but know you are not alone. The women we interviewed are all like you – they all have or had successful careers and they all experienced a PCM. All were from different backgrounds, but once they recognised these moments and navigated through them, despite the experience of them being different and at times difficult and challenging, what they all had in common was they achieved greater career success when they worked past the moment than before.

One in particular was Eliza – a senior people and culture executive with over 25 years' experience across a range of industries, including financial services, professional services, IT and the resources sector. Eliza loved her job and company, and had a successful track record of project delivery, had built great relationships and had the support from the executive team and the board. However, things changed when a project went off track. Instead of seeing the problematic project as a learning opportunity, her CEO lost confidence in Eliza's ability – and they never moved past it. Trust eroded and the relationship suffered. Eliza became a completely different person. She started second-guessing her decisions, avoiding certain situations, and not enjoying turning up to work. Her confidence snowball started to tumble. After a particularly difficult conversation with her boss, both agreed things had to change.

Once Eliza understood that she was experiencing a PCM, she gained a different perspective to what was happening. In her case, the best thing was to approach the scenario in a different way. Instead of trying to 'fix' things out of her control, she reframed the issues and focused on healing from the knocks and bruises of the dysfunctional relationship with her CEO. Eliza focused her energy on her strengths, knowledge and wisdom as she embarked on a six-month key delivery and handover plan. She focused on the positive relationships with other key stakeholders within the business. She regained trust in herself and her judgement and delivered some of her best work. Eliza removed herself from the negative scenario and regained her confidence through clarity on what she could control during this period. She then exited the job she had once loved. What we want to share is that Eliza did secure a new role and enjoys a new chapter in her successful career. We return to Eliza's story throughout this book.

Summing up

In this chapter, we've run through what confidence is and how women and men can perceive – and display – it differently. We've also discussed the impact of our labels or our self-talk. We seem to take comfort in collecting labels and labelling – for example, the imposter syndrome label. A comfort in the collective comes when we talk about the feelings behind such labels together. However, labelling can happen unconsciously, and we need to bring this to our conscious thoughts to redirect and challenge the neural pathway habits that are forming. What we believe and what we tell ourselves will be true. We need to fact check.

We also need to change our relationship with confidence by revisiting those original definitions about trust in ourselves. We need to stay true to that definition and not compare ourselves to unrealistic standards or confidence behaviours set by others. Start listening to yourself. Understand your narrative and how to challenge this and reframe. Start to adopt a mindset that embraces vulnerability and builds your resilience. Not doing so, and instead allowing your confidence to keep taking hit after hit, is what can lead to the snowball effect that rolls you into a PCM – which we cover in the next chapter.

2

Pivotal career moments

You may not control all events that happen to you,
but you can decide not to be reduced by them.
Maya Angelou

Over our collective decades of working directly with senior executives, we've discovered that during key professional and personal moments, a phenomenon exists that has the potential to derail careers. This phenomenon can turn up in many different ways and, in our experience, tends to impact women more significantly than men. As we've already introduced, we call these 'pivotal career moments' (PCMs), and they can play a massive role in your confidence and ability to achieve success. A bad experience during a PCM can cripple your confidence and lead to feelings of self-doubt and inadequacy.

In this chapter, we introduce you to what those moments are so that you can understand when you're heading towards – or going through – one. We walk you through how PCMs relate to your confidence, and how they can, if not understood or navigated through, ultimately create not just a confidence snowball but also a career avalanche. We outline the kinds of thoughts and feelings you're likely to feel during a PCM and start to identify some ways to bust that snowball, covering the planning and preparation needed now to navigate through these moments.

Defining pivotal career moments

As mentioned, PCMs are events or decisions that have a significant impact on your career trajectory. In this moment, you are faced with a choice or an opportunity that could potentially change the course of your professional and/or personal life. These events are either in or, more likely, out of your control – in your career or life, separately or even at the same time, with that event negatively affecting your confidence. We are not talking about smaller day-to-day issues that can be managed; we are talking about the big, unexpected ones that can have a profound impact on your professional journey and can shape the direction of your career for years to come.

A PCM can serve as a turning point in your career or life journey, and can shape and influence your goals and aspirations. Perhaps your role is made redundant, you are transitioning to a different role or a new job, have a new boss, or are going through a corporate restructure, or you've experienced a setback, failure or some form of discrimination. On a personal level, you may be going through a relationship change or a divorce, looking after ageing parents, or dealing with a health or wellbeing issue. For women in their mid to late 40s, in many cases the trigger for a PCM can be perimenopause or menopause. Unfortunately, breast cancer can also turn up as the top health issue for women today. Today, for men, it's prostate cancer.

Examples of events leading to a PCM for the women we interviewed included:

- restructure resulting in a redundancy

- corporate takeover resulting in a new boss, with different style and values
- marriage breakdown
- business venture not going well, resulting in financial distress
- speaking up about a project failure and that feedback was not received well by stakeholders
- corporate restructure, resulting in a new CEO
- COVID-19 creating a period of self-reflection on values and purpose
- being overlooked for a job promotion and new opportunity
- health and wellbeing deteriorating – burnout, perimenopause and illness
- returning to work from parental leave to a new boss who was not supportive of flexible work arrangements.

These PCMs all led to a drop in confidence for our interviewees, and while the impact on each individual varied, collectively the negative impacts of these PCMs included an overall feeling of disappointment.

We want to note at this point that you will have positive experiences in your career that act as confidence boosters, such as having your contributions recognised and rewarded, getting a promotion or getting additional responsibilities. These moments likely make you feel valued and energised, and are wonderful moments for growth and development. The PCMs we cover in this book are not these moments. We are talking about the negative ones. Our experience and our research demonstrate that these negative events are linked to, and are likely to cause, a sudden erosion of confidence. If not addressed, they will cause a career avalanche – and this is what we want to help women avoid. As we outlined in chapter 1 (and cover in more detail in the next chapter), confidence can be influenced by a variety of factors – including personality traits, upbringing and previous experiences. We specifically want to explore the effect a PCM has on your confidence because PCMs can be significantly impact-ful, and involve important decisions and events that can shape your career trajectory and sense of self-worth.

PCMs are significant because they involve 'big life events' that affect your thoughts, feelings and emotions. They can have an impact on your behaviours and your ability to perform your job or continue with the accountabilities that you had previously. How you navigate your career through that moment is critical for your ongoing suc-cess. When these big moments start to appear, your first response is likely to enter fight, flight or freeze mode (more on this in the next section). Next, you might start assessing your value, second-guessing how you acted and what decisions you can make. You start to ques-tion your value and your ability to perform. You start to think, *Why is this happening to me now?*

These kinds or reactions and thoughts can lead to feelings of frustration, disillusionment and demotivation. PCMs also lead to increased levels of stress, particularly if they involve a high degree of uncertain risk. This stress can take a further toll on your mental health and overall wellbeing. Ultimately, the pressure to succeed and excel during a PCM can lead to burnout, particularly if you don't have the resources or strategies to support you.

As mentioned in chapter 1, the stories we are sharing are from executive women who have successfully navigated their PCM. Some have continued to work in large corporate environments, and some have decided to leave corporate roles and start up their own busi-nesses and are pursuing a new chapter that satisfies their work–life goals. Going it alone takes courage. Both of us – Vanessa in her coaching experience and Marianne in the banking and wealth man-agement sector – have seen women making choices about their own business to escape corporate life. They've hit the ceiling or found the environment incompatible or both – experiencing a clash of values, stifling personal goals and a lack of flexibility, just to name a few.

Any career decision requires clarity, and this is why you need to explore your journey and relationship with confidence, especially during a PCM, to make sure that you are not unconsciously avoiding, stopping actively seeking or saying no to circumstances that could change or enhance your career opportunities. Another important factor to remember is that this lack of confidence experienced during a PCM can come as a surprise. The women we interviewed had described having high levels of confidence in the past; however, during a PCM, they lost it. We have both over our careers also seen this occur, and experienced it.

✎ Reflection point

Take a moment now to list your best career moments – the ones that you were most proud of.

When you're reflecting on these moments, think about your confidence levels and rate them from 1 to 10, with 10 being super confident, and 1 being low confidence.

Now think about what is happening in your career now.

Loss of confidence snowball and career avalanche

Understanding and navigating these pivotal moments is crucial – not only for your career but also for your wellbeing. When executives go through these PCMs, it rocks their confidence in making decisions, and has a negative impact on their wellbeing. Our research showed this is a harsh reality faced by many executive women. Some of the women we interviewed still found recalling the impact their PCMs had on their confidence and wellbeing difficult. They described it as a crippling emotional blow, but all wanted to share their experience to let other people, mainly women, learn from them and not feel alone.

Our research also highlighted how a PCM can turn into a career avalanche. As stress and anxiety builds up, rocking our confidence further, we begin second-guessing our decisions and start to lose control of things that were previously in our direct control. Our confidence falls even more, and the worst impact of this can be that careers fall away unexpectedly – which can be a lonely, isolating and devastating situation. This is the main aim of this book – to help and support women in these moments. With the right support, you can turn the event around.

In Vanessa's coaching experience, women can present initially as traumatised following a PCM. The emotional struggle with self-doubt, anxiety and stress brought on by the experience is palpable. While allowing women a safe environment to explore their feelings, Vanessa observes a sense of suffocation, exhaustion and bruising from the tumbling effects of this downward spiral. This is serious. As executive women lose their confidence, they also lose sight of themselves and lose their trust in themselves.

Interestingly, an outward projection of confidence is often still important to women. The executive women we interviewed were happy to share their stories to help and support other women, but in some cases didn't want to be personally named, because they were concerned about what others might think if they were not seen to be confident. All of us, ourselves included, in this demographic have fought a long career battle to gain a seat at the table. Our nervousness in suggesting we don't have it all under control is warranted.

The confidence snowball isn't a pleasant experience. As identified in our research, feelings during this time include anxiety, stress, nervousness, demotivation, procrastination, negativity and uncertainty. This stressful experience can trigger a neurobiological response. We mentioned the fight, flight or freeze response earlier. This is an automatic physiological and hormonal response to something we perceive as threatening or frightening. The limbic system – the emotional centre in our brain detecting fear and associated memories – takes over in an attempt to keep us safe.

Not only does this state feel unpleasant, but we also have limited access to our optimal brain power. Our ability to think strategically and rationally, problem-solve and make decisions can be reduced. This isn't a great state to be in – and we cover its effect on your health in chapter 5. Challenging thoughts, unpleasant memories and anecdotal evidence reinforced by constant negative self-talk prove and reinforce our negative theories. A collection of snowballs can create a career avalanche where, at worst, we can feel completely buried as the world comes crashing down around us.

Let's explore this idea of the avalanche a little.

Whistler Blackcomb is the largest and most popular ski resort in Canada and is a place we have visited. What we discovered was before the resort opens each day, hazard prevention teams assess the terrain, and we would often wake up to the sound of avalanche control blasting. These are powerful explosions that are designed to challenge the potentially unstable terrain, blowing up masses of snow identified as potential avalanche risks to help prevent a disaster. Experts assess the area using avalanche danger scales and data from high-frequency pressure sensors.

For those adventure seekers and risk-takers who prefer back country snow over the groomed trails, additional individual preparation is recommended. Even if the terrain appears to be fine, safety standards designed by seasoned experts recommend that skiers and snowboarders away from the main trails take extra precautions by wearing an avalanche airbag. This avalanche airbag is designed to prevent the wearer from being buried in an avalanche and has been reported to improve the chance of survival by 50 per cent.

Similarly, you need to take action to stop the metaphorical loss of confidence snowball rolling out of control and causing you to get caught in a career avalanche. Identifying the first stages of danger – the negative thoughts and feelings, the doubts – can help you start to take action.

Someone who knows all about this is Yasmin – CEO of a high-profile Australian industry body with a career in senior corporate and regulatory affairs, media and government relations, and C-suite roles in the media and entertainment sector, as well as non-executive and advisory roles. She is used to leading change and dealing with political environments. However, certain events started to undermine her confidence (setting off the confidence snowball). She started questioning her decisions and her approach, and doubting herself. She wasn't conscious of her confidence eroding and her anxiety and stress increasing until it was too late.

Yasmin described to us the perfect avalanche. In our interview, we discussed the moments in her career that had shaken her confidence, and whether she had allowed these moments to gather momentum and snowball, or if she dealt with them, busting them apart early. As she reflected on her high-profile C-suite position, she realised she had felt some early warning signs but had ignored them, instead blaming herself. Snowballs love gathering up all negativity as they gain momentum, including blame. During her PCM, Yasmin continued to question herself and doubt her ability. For a highly intelligent, accomplished executive leader, this shift was painful and crippling. Snowballs on multiple fronts gathered momentum and, ultimately, her career avalanche occurred, leaving her feeling buried and overwhelmed. The sad reality is this is a common story among executive women. In Yasmin's case, she negotiated an exit package and took some time to recover from the emotional and physical toll this career avalanche took on her and her family. We provide more on Yasmin's learning journey in chapter 7.

The more momentum the loss in confidence snowball gathers, the more difficult it is to control. We must understand the important link between confidence and self-compassion. We need to nurture ourselves and create the right environment so that we can bust the loss of confidence snowball before it creates a career avalanche. Understanding and acknowledging our feelings and emotions is important. Psychologist Dr Susan David is an authority on what she calls *emotional agility*. She describes how tapping into our emotions, naming our feelings, and leaning into challenging situations with curiosity, kindness and self-compassion can reconnect us to our values and how we really desire to show up. We see a connection between Dr David's findings and the confidence snowball we describe. Leaning into feelings and emotions early can help you choose your pathway forward – and bust the snowball before the momentum takes hold.

✎ Reflection point

Thinking about your previous reflections on your career and now that you have learnt more about PCMs, could you be in or heading towards a PCM?

Can you recognise the tipping points that have changed your confidence?

Thoughts and feelings for women during PCMs

Understanding your feelings and thoughts during a PCM is so important. As already outlined, our research demonstrated that during these moments, the biggest impact on any individual was on their confidence. For the executives we talked with, the experience derailed their ability to think clearly and assess what was happening to them. It also clouded their ability to make the key decisions they needed to help them succeed.

Research also suggests that men and women can experience PCMs differently due to the presence of gender biases and stereotypes in the workplace. We cover this more in detail in chapter 11, but for now understand that women face barriers to advancement and recognition due to gender-based discrimination and bias, and this can make it more difficult for women to achieve the same level of success as their male counterparts, even when they possess similar skills and qualifications.

Our research showed the effect of a PCM for women was greater than it was for men. While men often took this moment 'on the chin' and moved through the moment faster, women were less able to get through the moment as quickly, and their ability to learn and grow from the scenario was reduced. In some cases, their ability to make decisions that worked for them was crippled. The impact of the PCM was profound. All of a sudden, this person showed up differently and acted differently.

An example of this is Susan, a strategic C-suite technology executive. Susan has managed large-scale IT operations across an international footprint, and led complex digital transformation project portfolios within fast moving consumer goods (FMCG), retail, financial services and management consulting industries. She shared her experience following the appointment of a new boss, a change in her workload, and a shift in the corporate culture. These combined to create a PCM for Susan, reducing her confidence and causing changes in her behaviour. However, Susan was initially unaware of this impact, and it was a colleague who brought the situation to her attention. They noticed a change in how she showed up during a presentation. Susan was known for being energetic, and a confident and capable executive; however, her colleague noticed that she was more reserved, and appeared uncomfortable during this presentation. This prompted the feedback, 'You are turning up differently.'

Your behaviour is different.' At the time, Susan couldn't make the connection. It wasn't until she allowed more in-depth self-reflection that she understood she was experiencing a PCM.

The impact of this confidence crisis on the wellbeing and decisions of the female executives we spoke to ranged from a struggle to a disaster. Our research showed that, for many women, PCMs adversely impact or derail current problem-solving and decision-making, and even weaken future decisions. They can stop women from taking on new challenges, and these new challenges are sometimes critical to their future success. Women can be so derailed by PCMs and their decision-making so shaken that they can make decisions not in their best interests, which in the worst case can impact career success and potentially stifle their financial wellbeing. In this context, wealth accumulation is important so women can achieve financial independence, to attain their goals and dreams, during their working life and in retirement.

Reducing confidence isn't the only factor holding women back, of course. But when we shared our stories, we found similarities that were reinforced by our research.

Another similarity we uncovered through our research was that successful female executives at the top of their game often personalise the event when a PCM happens. They think it's only happening to them. This also impedes or derails their future decision-making. Our research shows that a PCM can happen to anybody – and it's happened to lots of people. However, women's tendency to personalise the situation impacts them in different ways. For some, the impact was felt most strongly in their wellbeing and health; for others, it was in a loss of networks or relationships. Or it could be a combination of a number of issues. What this tells us is that PCMs – and the resulting snowball effect on women's confidence – can happen to anybody and everybody at some stage. It may happen once or multiple times.

Even people who, from an external perspective, seemed to be the most confident people were still struggling during these PCMs.

Cognitive distortions often come into play in your thinking during PCMs, and these are the derailers of confidence. Understanding the factors that contribute to derailing your confidence – including your thoughts and feelings – can help you put strategies in place to prepare you for this moment more successfully. This understanding can not only help you in that PCM, but also help you navigate through that moment more quickly. Then you can learn from this experience, move past the moment and continue on your successful career.

Taking the time to understand your feelings and thoughts can also help you understand the relationship between your feelings and thoughts and those things that are both in and out of your control. Listing the things that are in your control can help you focus on those issues and reduce cognitive distortions, which in turn helps you make decisions and problem-solve with more clarity. Listing the things outside your control can help you isolate them and so reduce focus, energy and stress about those issues.

We interviewed Sally, an entrepreneur, business owner and author with 30 years' experience across the financial services and media industries. Sally shared with us that she had made some decisions that didn't land the way that she wanted. These decisions had huge financial consequences. To overcome them, she had to reinvent and recreate her whole life – including selling the family home and relocating to a new area, away from family and friends, and her children having to change schools. What got Sally through this moment was her understanding of which aspects of the situation she could control – and which she couldn't. She navigated through those issues and tried to create a positive experience for her family. She's now rebuilding her wealth, but taking with her the learnings from that experience – not just for her but also for her whole family.

✏ Reflection point

How are you feeling? What are you thinking? Are these thoughts and feelings having an impact on other parts of your life? Usually, the first impact is to sleep and your mood. Is that changing?

People around you – friends or colleagues – may be noticing that you're behaving differently. Are they asking questions about that? Questions from colleagues and friends can be a good indicator of whether you're in a PCM.

Bringing your own stories and strategies to a conscious level will build resilience for future PCMs.

Busting snowballs

Too many executive women's careers get derailed. When you're in one of those negative spirals, your confidence crisis can snowball. Personalising it, catastrophising it and allowing cognitive distortions to creep in will create the snowball effect that will continue to erode your confidence and affect your decision-making if you don't get on top of it. Being in this state can be crippling – and not just to your current career, but also to your future decision-making. It's important for women to recognise the signs of a PCM and avoid that snowball and the career avalanche.

Remember – a PCM can happen to anyone, and it has happened to lots of different people. Our research focused on successful executives who then experienced this moment, and how it rocked their confidence. At this point in time, they had choices to make. Understanding the relationship between the confidence crisis and the PCM helped them navigate a way forward to continue to have a successful career.

At a micro level, we heard many stories of a PCM having a negative impact. Women couldn't get out of that negative cycle and that then stopped them from taking on different roles or held them back from successful careers. At a macro level, female executives dealing with PCMs can have an impact on future decisions. Our research showed that these moments had the potential to stop women taking on new challenges and jobs. This macro-level impact plays into the gender pay gap, and plays a role in fewer women being in C-suite or executive roles. We want to bust this snowball and help people navigate through so that they can continue to have successful careers. (See chapter 11 for more on the macro impact.)

✎ Reflection point

Has there ever been a time where a lack of confidence hindered you in taking a career opportunity? If your answer is 'yes', you are like so many others.

Understanding this connection between confidence and taking up opportunities is important. Note down how you were feeling and your thinking during this time.

Planning and preparing

If you are in or heading towards a PCM, what can you do now? Having a plan and a prepared approach will help you navigate through a PCM. We've seen it in our research and we've heard it in the stories of women who have navigated these successfully. When they have moved through them, they have offered valuable opportunities for learning and growth, both personally and professionally.

Experiencing a PCM can feel overwhelming, daunting and crippling. But know that you can move through it. Strategies can help you. Planning and preparing is going to be your key to success, and we'll delve into that in more detail later.

For now, know that you can get through this moment in time. We both have! Vanessa has been coaching executives through this moment for almost 20 years. She has great success in meeting an individual and recognising that they're in a PCM. Through executive coaching, she has been able to help them navigate through their personal journey.

Marianne experienced her own PCM, and the support of her network and her executive coach helped her step outside and not personalise the situation, which helped her prepare and think about the strategies to move through it. Being able to prepare and strategise helped her move through the experience a lot faster and learn from it. Marianne's key learnings included greater self-awareness of the strengths that helped her navigate her career path, building more resilience, and improving her adaptability. The PCM helped her think more creatively about future possibilities, and this opened new networks and opportunities.

Reflection point

Think about your career. Do you have goals? Have you got a career plan? Everything starts with a good plan, and starting early will help you drive confidence. Start thinking now about your goals. Getting to a PCM with some idea of your goals will help you develop a plan, a structure and an approach. This can help you move through that moment more quickly.

Summing up

PCMs can happen to anybody, and they've happened to many senior executives in top roles. PCM triggers can vary and will depend on a range of factors. When you're in that moment, recognise that some things are in your control and some are out of your control. You have learnt that a link exists between the impact of that moment and your confidence. The experience can go from a struggle to feeling quite disastrous. At the disastrous level, the erosion of your confidence can have a negative snowball effect – exactly what we are trying to avoid. We want to give you strategies and the confidence to know that you can navigate through that moment more quickly and be able to continue with your successful career.

Start to understand the relationship between your thoughts and feelings. What cognitive distortions or negative thinking patterns are at play for you? How are they showing up?

Do not personalise a situation. How you choose to respond to your PCM is in your control. Learn from the situation and think about your plan and preparation.

We've spoken about confidence, and we've introduced PCMs and how these can derail your confidence and lead to negative snowball effects. Strategies are available to help you navigate these pivotal moments, and we explore these in much more detail in parts II and III. In the next chapter, we discuss confidence levels over different stages of your career.

3

Career stage, confidence and pivotal career moments

The courageous conversation is the one you don't want to have.
David Whyte

Your confidence can change over the decades of your career, and the first couple of decades can have a huge influence on confidence levels. However, as the decades progress, the stakes get higher. Executives we interviewed had a series of career changes throughout their lives – from moving to different roles in the same company to being employed in a variety of organisations across industry sectors.

We also found our risk assessment processes change as we grow in our careers. In this book, risk means what you're prepared to give up, or the additional risk you're willing to take on when entering your next life stage. When you think about risk, perhaps you define it as a situation involving exposure to danger. We're also talking about how you interpret that danger. Your perception of risk could be a threat to your identity, your income, your status level or how comfortable you feel in your role. It could also be perceived as a threat to your relationships, further opportunities, the environment you work in, and your work–life balance.

In this chapter, we discuss the impact of confidence on risk-taking at various life and career stages, and how the narrative from your upbringing and environment can still affect your confidence lens today – hindering or helping during pivotal career moments (PCMs). Your career risk appetite can change at each life stage, so we also explore the importance of reassessing and resetting your career goals and expectations at each stage. Finally, we look at the importance of redefining your purpose, values and passions, and how this can build confidence during a PCM.

Impact of upbringing – nature and nurture in motion

Let's explore the impact of upbringing and environment on confidence levels. In our survey, for the question, 'Where does your confidence come from?', 27.5 per cent selected 'Born with it' and/or 'From parents and upbringing'. This figure – just over a quarter of respondents – is not significantly high. However, in our follow-up interviews when we asked, 'Where do you think confidence comes from?', all interviewees spoke to their childhood, their upbringing, and how this affected their sense of self and related confidence levels.

Some were surprised about this impact when reflecting. It had been some time since childhood, but for many it felt like only yesterday. Fast-forward to today, and the impact is still as strong. A questioning parent or carer can still bring on a feeling of self-doubt or, for others, a sense of reassurance and belief in themselves. Some of our interviewees still wrestle with unachievable standards and expectations.

We introduced Emma in chapter 1. In her interview, she defined confidence as 'Being able to feel worthwhile and withstand criticism'.

This pricked our curiosity about the impact her parents may have played on her confidence journey. She went on to tell us about her parents not wanting her to have a 'big head', meaning not to have a big ego, and how this peppered her confidence during her early career, sowing the seeds for ongoing doubt. These doubts continue still to this day – in a recent conversation with her mother about an event where Emma was presenting, her mother asked Emma, 'Why would anyone want to listen to you?' Emma attempted to rationalise this. 'On one hand, she's probably curious – like, what on earth do you talk about?' But Emma was also quick to provide another interpretation – a less than positive one that felt belittling and was hardwired in her mind.

Childhood and upbringing can tell us a lot about how we apply pre-programmed mindsets to executive careers, our confidence story and the journey along the way.

Our interviewee Victoria, a chief operating officer with deep experience in leading transformation through mergers and acquisitions in the financial services sector, described her upbringing in an academic family. She felt loved and supported but also felt like she didn't quite fit in. She was average at school academically while her siblings and her parents soared in the academic world. One thing she did excel in was ongoing self-judgement. She felt she didn't meet expectations. However, once she tapped into and embraced her differences to her family in a positive way that acknowledged her own strengths, the shackles came off. Her confidence and career flourished.

✐ Reflection point

Think of the story of your upbringing. What are the narratives you created around this time? What parts of this have you recreated? What hardwired beliefs make this narrative so powerful for you? How do these narratives play out?

Confidence varies through life stages and decades

Each life stage brings its own milestones and challenges. You may think that for most people, confidence increases over time – with the pinnacle achieved during the wisdom of our 50s and 60s as we age gracefully. Our experience and research shows this is not always the case for executive women. We found some distinct differences between each decade, and this was a foundational motivator for us writing this book.

Post-university, or straight to work from school for some, our interviewees shared that they had an acceptance of not knowing everything, as well as being comfortable in situations where they were 'thrown into the deep end' – which allowed them to fail fast and learn at that time. For some, confidence dipped in these early career years, while for others confidence grew through these experiences and challenges. Eliza, from chapter 1, recalled her early nickname – 'Miss Colgate', from early toothpaste television commercials, because she had a 'ring of confidence'.

We then springboard through our 20s and into our 30s, and some described having partners and children during this time. For some, they found it comforting to have people in their corner to support them in building and consolidating their career. Others described having greater freedom and flexibility to explore their career and the world. For most, this was a period when they were starting to earn more money.

Then we move into the years of the 40s, where we found that decisions made during this time set up the career level for most of the women who were currently at executive level. This was a time where career purpose and meaning met capability and experience. This time often also included those PCMs brought on by factors such as young children, relationship impacts, needing to firm up decisions about family future, reducing the family flexibility and women opting out of executive careers. Many found the popular images of women being able to juggle everything to be fictitious and, without many examples of other female executives around them, found it hard to be what they couldn't see.

As they moved into their 50s, some women we spoke with described it as a time where wisdom and experience weren't always acknowledged or recognised. The George Clooney–style grey hair may work well for men, but signs of ageing became limiting for some women. Health issues also entered the equation, as well as those natural cycles of life, often not talked about – for example, meno-pause. (We discuss this important topic in chapter 5.) While younger children require closer hands-on care and attention, sometimes the bigger the children, the bigger the problems to worry about – as chil-dren moved into their teenage and young adult years, issues relating to aspects such as drinking, drugs, driving, relationships and career all started to emerge. Throw ageing parents on top and the sandwich generation that occurs during our 40s and 50s can create PCMs – and predominantly for women, who still provide a larger proportion of unpaid care.

The experience in our 50s and 60s is when the results of our survey data really became interesting. Nervousness and negative self-talk were the most common impacts of low confidence on women, regardless of age. However, age is a distinguisher for both – younger women are more likely to feel nervous, while older women are more likely to be self-critical. Overall, impacts were more common – and more severe – the older in age our interviewees were. This indicates the impact of low confidence appears to be related to age. Older women were twice as likely to say their confidence came from their parents or upbringing. Despite being more likely to be self-critical, older women were more likely to find positive thinking helpful when confidence is low. Lack of expertise, knowledge or skill was a source of confidence erosion for almost 75 per cent of the older women we spoke with; however, they were also more likely to address skill and capability gaps independently. Younger women, on the other hand, were more likely to seek help from their support crew or ask a mentor and to jump in and act. This highlights some clear differences in coping mechanisms by age bracket.

Each decade of life brings a different story and influences the expectations that we set. Embracing what we learn, what we need to let go and how we can move on is important. If we can learn from each decade but not compare ourselves across the decades, we can embrace this as an ongoing time to grow and to learn. Our ability to do this will either build or bust our confidence.

✐ **Reflection point**

Reflect on your career. In your journal, map your career and confidence journey throughout the decades. Which moments stand out as impactful? Where are those imprinted, stressful, anxiety-filled moments? Sit with these for a while. What impact have these moments had on your current confidence? Have you resolved this? Can you look at this through a different lens? What additional help do you need to resolve this? What would you tell that younger version of yourself now? What advice would you give them?

Our upbringing still impacts our confidence lens today

The narrative from our upbringing can still affect our confidence lens today. Societal aspects, such as gender biases growing up, still have an impact on executive women today. Challenging these biases requires resilience, which can in turn challenge our confidence. Personal aspects, such as the stories and the actions from our parents and family, can also be hardwired in these formative years. These are part of our identity. Our parents, upbringing and family have been influential in our lives.

Amelia, from chapter 1, provided a great example of this. She reminisced about the hardwired narrative she'd internalised from her parents: 'Don't start something unless you are going to do it properly'. Upon reflection and when asked what advice she'd give to her younger self, she realised she wished she'd understood the notion of the 'desire' to do things perfectly versus 'being able' to do them all perfectly all the time. She realises now she'd focused more on the latter, with its ensuing unrealistic expectation levels of perfectionism.

While on the topic of perfectionism, an (unnamed) executive woman quoted in the KPMG 2020 Women's Leadership Summit Report, *Advancing the Future of Women in Business*, sums it up:

> I am a recovering perfectionist, so failures are difficult to forget.
> I am working on recovering faster from perceived failures and being much more forgiving of my humanness.

We discuss self-compassion further in chapter 7. For now, spend some time trying to understand, assess and challenge the actions, limitations and questions you've placed on yourself, which still affect your confidence today.

From a generational perspective, Vanessa's mother had to leave her job at the English, Scottish & Australian (ES&A) Bank when she got married at 21. (ES&A Bank had a network of 570 branches across Australia when it merged with ANZ in 1970 to form Australia and New Zealand Banking Group Limited.) She had to leave once she was married because of the assumption that she was now being looked after by her husband. It seems so archaic that someone, with such capability, was forced out of the workforce due to marital status. Later, Vanessa's mother didn't have the confidence to re-enter the corporate workforce. Instead, she decided to become a hairdresser, and bought Camelot Hair Fashions and undertook her apprenticeship.

In her early 50s, Vanessa's mother did go on to educate herself in the investment community, attend courses at the Australian Stock Exchange, and learn how to do investment charting and modelling. She established and managed the family investments and superannuation portfolio – providing a great example of reinvention, reskilling and upskilling, regardless of age. A lifetime of corporate income lost because of employment conditions was slowly regained due to her determination, resilience and newly acquired investment knowledge. However, the lessons imparted to Vanessa – 'play it safe, get a secure job, keep your head down and you'll have a job for life' – had an influence that needed to be acknowledged and worked through. Vanessa's mother's story of financial reinvention is also not the case for all women, even today, as we continue to see the divide between male and female wealth creation and the dire future for some women (more on this in chapter 11).

✏ Reflection point

What are the stories, quotes and comments you remember from your upbringing? Write down any 'pearls of wisdom' in your journal. How have you taken this on? How do you interpret them? What feelings do you have when you recall these stories? What behaviours have ensued from the stories from your upbringing? Think about Amelia's example in this section and how she was able to think of another perspective. Are you able to do the same?

Our career risk appetite changes over time

Our career risk appetite changes at each life stage, highlighting the importance of reassessing and resetting our career goals and expectations. In a younger decade risk assessment, the stakes are generally lower, and more risks may be taken. With each increasing decade, and as factors such as family investment and financial commitments increase, the stakes become higher and fewer risks may be taken.

When we get to empty nesters, financial commitments settle, the stakes start to reduce and there are different types of risks.

Determining the criteria for career risk assessment can build confidence in your decisions and judgement throughout your career, and give you confidence to trust yourself in your decisions.

When we interviewed Kiara, a C-level executive with a passion for digital, media and tech-oriented businesses, and group chief financial officer of an ASX-listed company, she reflected back over her career choices and judged herself as not taking enough risks. She described how early in her career journey – particularly in her 20s and 30s, when 'ignorance is bliss' – she took more risks. You don't think (or don't know) of the ramifications of what you're doing, so taking these risks seems fine. In her 40s, however, Kiara started to become a lot more stable and put more safeguards in place – and, looking back, described her choices as a bit boring. This started her doubt and questioning again, as she put pressure on herself and judged herself, saying 'I should have taken more risks'.

This judgement was undermining her confidence in her decisions for future roles. Her narrative of the past – which was that she should have done better, taken more risks, worked internationally – needed to be built on a more holistic acceptance of herself. Her life had changed. An approach that may have been seen as not taking enough risk earlier in her career was more suited for where her career was at now. After resetting her goals, this became clearer. As Kiara said, 'You need to draw a line in the sand and move from there'. Accepting a chief financial officer role in an ASX-listed organisation was a bold, ambitious goal that required stretch; however, the role was in Australia, with a supportive CEO and executive team, and enabled her to have the flexibility to manage a young family.

Kiara's experience aligns with many executives Vanessa has worked with. A common issue is that executives who haven't revisited their holistic goals often don't have a sense of identity that is clear or of value to them. They are unclear about what defines their purpose and meaning. They base their next role on goals of the past, not what they need for the future. We provide strategies on addressing this in chapter 7 but, for now, we want you to know that coaching is a great way to assist in any goal re-identification required.

You can start by using our Multifactor Risk-Assessment matrix, provided in table 1. Across the top of the matrix, we've included possible life stage factors that may influence a career decision. In the second column, we've listed possible career options you may be considering (you can also add your own). For each of the career options you're considering, you can then rate how important each of the life stage factors is when making your decision – with a rating of 1 being least important and a rating of 6 being highly important. These ratings can help you decide whether or not the career option might be right for you.

When thinking about your goals and career options and completing the matrix, also work through the following:

- What is your definition of success and happiness?
- What life stage you are at now?
- What do 'identity' and 'purpose' mean to you in this life stage?
- What does a 'balanced' life looks like for you?
- What lifestyle do you want now and for the next stage of your life?
- What does 'ego' mean to you?

✎ Reflection point

The Multifactor Risk-Assessment matrix enables you to look at current and future life stages while overlaying future career goals. What's important now? What do you desire for the future? Test whether you are hanging onto old life stage narratives. Where is the tension between what was then and what is now?

Table 1: Multifactor Risk-Assessment matrix

Career option being considered	Life stage factors							
	Family (age and stage)	Identity, purpose, meaning	Holistic balance and wellbeing	Ego	Lifestyle	Financial goals	Location and required travel	Relationships
Own business/entrepreneur								
Portfolio career								
Start-up organisation								
Corporate (ASX-listed company)								
Corporate (private company)								
Not-for-profit/charity organisation								
Other options								

Pivotal career moments and confidence anchor points

If you don't challenge the pre-programmed notions about your career and reframe the narrative from your youth, inaction can start a downward confidence snowball. If you don't acknowledge the life stages that you've experienced, confidence may dip further as you unconsciously assess yourself against goal posts set for earlier career or life stages. Those goals might not be relevant to the life stage that you're in now.

We've found that many executives don't revisit, review or reset their holistic life and career objectives. They can be plagued by, 'I should have done this', or 'I must (or have to) do this', versus what they *want* to do at that stage. Be aware that the disconnect between what you should do and what you want to do can create the perfect conditions for a confidence crisis. You need to be aware of all these factors to navigate a crisis of confidence that can be caused by a PCM, and put what we call 'confidence anchor points' in place.

As Vanessa reflected on her upbringing, she realised her loving parents wanted a safe and secure work environment for her. They encouraged her to pursue safe, secure work options and not take risks. Career conversations early on revolved around a public sector clerical role – where you could keep your head down and, if lucky enough, have a job for life! Long tenure rated highly. This risk-mitigation approach didn't encourage her to open the door to a world of career opportunities. Vanessa pushed back because she knew this wasn't aligned to her motivation, and started a career in nursing. Coupled with this choice, Vanessa's other early ambition for a singing career emerged. So, a few years after graduating as a registered nurse, she made a career change and left the nursing profession. This decision was met with disappointment from her parents – why leave a secure vocation? So, Vanessa decided to transfer her skills to a corporate career and undertake further study and combine this with her singing career. The narratives 'you always need something to fall back on' and 'play it safe' were hardwired.

Across this time, she released three records (including the first digitally recorded single in Australia), signed a television contract and was awarded three times as Queensland's female entertainer of the year, performing nationally and internationally. She juggled her singing and corporate career, working in some cases seven days and nights a week. Juggling everything in this way was not sustainable. She was very young and for the most part felt invincible, but the ingrained narrative of 'play it safe' was still plaguing her. As time went on, she gained perspective on the reality of her situation and let go of her professional singing career and focused on her corporate career, undertaking further postgraduate studies. She set new goals for her career, taking elements of what she loved and transferring this in a more secure environment. Initially she moved into sales, and then training and development enabled her to present and facilitate, bringing in some of that passion to perform and engage audiences. Then she moved into human resources, where she could align her purpose and passion for developing people strategies with helping the business transform and achieve success. She moved into senior executive roles, with more PCMs to come.

Marianne has also reflected on the influence of her upbringing. She is a first-generation Australian, with parents who both migrated to Australia – her dad for better economic prosperity and her mum for a new adventure and opportunities. Such a move takes courage, hard work and determination. Her father worked on the Snowy Mountains Scheme and had a career in the building industry, working on many landmarks across Sydney, Australia. Her mum had careers across aged care, fashion and retail. Since her childhood, Marianne's parents instilled in her and her siblings strong family values of kindness, respect, honesty and integrity. They focused on the importance of education and financial independence. While it was a strict upbringing, her parents always encouraged her and her siblings to be and do the best they could and never limit themselves to stereotypical norms or the current state of structures or processes. They supported their children and gave them confidence to be and achieve anything. Marianne and her siblings all went on to get university degrees and masters, with her sister building a career in education and her brother in banking and financial services.

For Marianne, this upbringing encouraged her to take on challenging and complex roles and jobs, and to continue studying (she's up to her third degree). It also encouraged Marianne to use her corporate position to advocate to improve things she felt were not right, such as gender inequity and the need for inclusive workplaces.

By 2020, Marianne had enjoyed a 25-year career, including a C-suite executive role in a large listed company in banking and financial services. She enjoyed her role, had a great team and serviced wonderful clients from across Australia, Hong Kong and Singapore. This role, however, also took Marianne away from her husband, two daughters and wider family most weeks. The onset of COVID-19, and working from home becoming the norm, and the sudden death of her brother-in-law at age 45, provided a reflection point for Marianne. Marianne took time out to reassess her purpose and goals. What she discovered was she wanted greater flexibility than a corporate structure could provide, so she could balance her ambitions with her family needs and wants. Marianne took time out to focus on the things she liked, while still having ambition, energy and drive to make a difference. With the support of her family, and her parents instilling courage and imagination, Marianne created a portfolio career. At the core of her vision for this new stage is her family and a focus on wellbeing. Her professional focus is then in three parts:

1. continuing to contribute to business, through non-executive directorships and advisory work

2. helping people reach their potential, through coaching and writing this book
3. contributing to the community through advocacy for workplace equality and inclusion, mental wellbeing and care for the planet.

This reflection highlighted the lessons learnt by both Vanessa and Marianne, and these lessons reinforced the need to have confidence anchor points. Not knowing what grounds us – that is, our values, passions, evolving goals and purpose – can leave us feeling adrift. Our brains are great prediction machines, designed to keep us safe. Uncertainty and ambiguity lead us to question ourselves. Questioning ourselves isn't a bad thing – it can help us reassess. However, negative inner chatter and unhelpful narratives from the past can set us off course and create perfect conditions for a declining confidence snowball.

Confidence anchor points stop us drifting off course. They include purpose, and the Cambridge dictionary states, 'if you do something on purpose, you do it intentionally, not by accident', and that purpose is 'determination or a feeling of having a reason for what you do'. Another confidence anchor point is your personal values – knowing what your values look like in action, and knowing when they are aligned or off course. Passion holds you firm. When you are passionate you feel drawn toward something, interested, excited and energised. And goals give you an anchor point, and a sense of knowing what you are aiming for.

All these confidence anchor points are foundational pieces in understanding your identity and you need to remind yourself constantly. Some executives have vision boards with pictures or images as a constant reminder of what's important, their values and the desired journey ahead. On her vision board, Marianne has a diagram outlining the three components of her work life mentioned in this section, and how they integrate purpose and meaning with her values. Vanessa has specific quotes that inspire her to continue her path.

Change happens in our lives that affects our identity. Importantly, executive life can inhibit the connection with our personal identity. Hence, at a pivotal point, executives can be knocked off balance. Redefining your purpose, values, passion and goals – creating these confidence anchor points – will build readiness for those PCMs.

✎ Reflection point

Are you clear on your purpose? Revisit your personal passions, purpose, vision and goals, and articulate these in a way that will be a reminder for you. Create a solid confidence anchor that will help ground you during PCMs and confidence snowballs.

What prompts you on a day-to-day basis?

Summing up

Each decade of your life brings additional layers and richness to your life experience. The imprint from your upbringing can be entrenched as motivating or demotivating. Embracing where you are right now and not competing against or being limited by your past can help boost confidence for the present and excitement for the journey ahead.

Change your career confidence lens to have an influence on the future as building on but not competing against the past. Our executive cohort clearly demonstrated how easy it is to allow the narrative of the past to have an impact today. In some cases, this was an unsettling impact; for others, it was a motivational reminder. Challenge the narrative from the past. Reassess its relevance to you. Identify your risk parameters for each stage of your career and create a new narrative. Look at what you've learned from your upbringing and early career. How can this motivate you in new and positive ways? Think about what you can control and can't control. You have control over what you choose to do with this information, for example.

In the chapters in this part, we've covered confidence and how it is impacted during PCMs and at different life and career stages. We've also introduced the concepts around our neurobiological stress response when we feel threatened, not safe or insecure (we expand on this in chapter 5). Let's continue this journey and delve further into environments that fuel this loss of confidence snowball. In the chapters in the next part, we uncover the evidence and research around psychological safety, health and wellbeing, and the impact your support crew can have on your confidence and your career.

PART II

Three key areas to focus on

4

Workplaces can kill your confidence

Corporate culture matters. How management chooses to treat its people impacts everything for better or worse.
Simon Sinek

Your workplace environment – and how psychologically safe it is – directly affects the confidence level of its employees. In the chapters in part I, we discussed confidence and how executive women describe it, the impact that a pivotal career moment (PCM) can have on confidence levels, and the snowball effect when confidence starts to plummet and stress and anxiety build. In this chapter, we unpack the important role psychologically safe workplace environments have on confidence, and the way corporate environments can have a damaging impact on confidence.

The psychological safety of the workplace (or lack thereof) was one of the key issues uncovered in our interviews and research. When our research participants experienced psychologically unsafe environments, this was a contributor to their PCM. On the other hand, workplaces of high psychological safety were a contributor to high performance and respondents' ability to bounce back from their PCMs.

The term 'psychological safety' was coined by Amy Edmondson. Edmondson is a Harvard Business School professor, and her work in this area has provided particular insight into how psychological safety plays out in corporate environments. She describes a psychologically safe work environment as one where people feel safe to speak up, share ideas and provide feedback, collaborate and take risks. In psychologically unsafe workplaces, people feel threats to their safety, their sense of self, their status or their position. If they engage in behaviours such as speaking up, giving feedback, discussing mistakes or taking accountability at times when things don't go as planned, they are made to feel unsafe. This was backed up by our research, which showed a key outcome of this type of environment is a negative impact on confidence.

It's important at this point to make a distinction between psychological safety and trust. You may be in a situation where you have a trusted relationship with your colleagues or peers, but still feel unsafe to speak up or share information in a group. This is because psychological safety focuses on how the group perceives a group norm. Trust focuses on how one person views another. When you are in a psychologically safe environment, you feel your colleagues will accept you for being your true self and not reject you for sharing your views, opinions or simply saying what you think. This environment is one of respect for each other, and one where you can constructively engage in conflict or confrontation as well as feel safe when you're trying new things or taking on risks. In this kind of environment, our interviewees worked at their best and were the most satisfied in their careers and personal lives.

This is why it is important to evaluate your corporate environment and understand how psychologically safe it is. If you don't, you are at risk of being in an unsafe environment that will impact your confidence and ability to be at your best. If you recognise this as a potential contributor to you experiencing a PCM, you can take action and overcome any obstacles stopping you from continuing on your successful career path.

In this chapter, we talk about how psychologically unsafe corporate environments are not conducive to executive women's optimal performance. We also cover how to recognise the early signs that you're in a psychologically unsafe corporate environment, which can enable you to implement coping strategies, or may involve developing skills such as political savviness. We show you how navigating corporate environments is a necessary skillset as a confidence enabler, and point out the importance of separating the things in your workplace environment that you can control from those that you can't. For the things that you can't control, you may need to consider some coping strategies to ensure the corporate environment does not cripple your confidence or impact your overall wellbeing. (We cover wellbeing in more detail in chapter 5.) Lastly, we look at how all leaders have the opportunity to reshape the future of corporate environments post the COVID-19 pandemic.

Executives perform their best in psychologically safe environments

Let's come back to our interviewee Eliza from part I, who was a people and culture executive in a large financial services organisation with a successful career when a situation occurred that Eliza's boss blamed Eliza for, and he couldn't let it go. The relationship between Eliza and her boss quickly changed. He became hypercritical of her, and this increased over time. This impacted her confidence. At the time, Eliza didn't understand the connection; instead, she started to pay more attention to his criticism and doubt her ability. Even with her negative self-talk coming in, for 12 months she tried to make it work. The relationship eventually became untenable, negatively affecting her performance because she was so focused on what her boss was criticising her for. She couldn't see through the feedback, and the resulting lack of confidence snowball impacted her both professionally and personally.

Through coaching and feedback from trusted colleagues, Eliza understood that she was in a PCM, and while she could focus on her own wellbeing, the environment and behaviours of her boss did not align to her values. These were factors she could not control, and eventually they led her to move on. What she learned was that her treatment by her boss was not an isolated experience. He created an environment that was psychologically unhealthy, where people couldn't speak up and were uncomfortable to admit when they didn't know things. Eliza's boss's behaviour created a blame culture that was not conducive to a learning culture.

This experience was a difficult one, and Eliza still feels the pain. She channels the learning from that situation to continually restate her values, what is important to her in a workplace environment, what she expects from any future leader, and how to ensure her own leadership style creates the right environment. She has since continued her successful career in a workplace that fosters a psychologically safe working environment.

Psychologically unsafe corporate environments are not conducive to anyone performing at their optimal level, but what we found from our research is that these environments have a worse impact on women. The experience of working, at an individual and organisational level, can have both a positive and negative impact on the level of your confidence, your motivation and your overall performance.

When we asked executive women to describe times in their career that they felt most confident, they described emotions such as passion, feeling deeply connected to their values and purpose, and feeling appreciated and valued. A common phrase they used was 'we could be our true selves'. They spoke of environments where they felt comfortable to make suggestions, try new things and take risks. They could operate from a growth mindset, as part of a high-performance team and performing at their peak. They told us when they felt a sense of flourishing in their work, this also extended to their personal lives. They connected this time in their careers to having a supportive boss and a psychologically safe working environment.

This is backed up by research from Google, which in 2016 conducted a two-year initiative focused on understanding what made a team work effectively. The number one dynamic in building a successful team was psychological safety.

Our research shows a direct link between workplace psychological safety and confidence. In environments of psychological safety, confidence is intact; conversely, confidence is crippled by work environments that are psychologically unsafe. In these environments, women described emotions of self-doubt, exhaustion, burnout, stress and strain.

A clear pattern is emerging here. Psychological safety in the workplace can help boost team morale and productivity, and improve retention and job satisfaction. Unsafe environments, on the other hand, have devastating impacts to career confidence and health. Given this direct linkage, what is most important for women in these situations is not to personalise the event and blame themselves.

In 2018, a global trend study by US-based consulting firm Mercer revealed that employees desire managerial support for their psychological and emotional wellbeing in the workplace. This finding is backed by our survey. When we asked participants, 'What erodes your confidence?', a staggering 85 per cent identified an unsupportive leader. Executives who we interviewed all told us that the moments in their careers that they felt most confident was when they had a supportive leader. The role leadership plays in ensuring a psychologically safe work environment is critical to its success. An example of this is Susan, who we introduced in chapter 2. Susan is a C-suite executive experienced in global technology who has managed large-scale IT operations across an international footprint and led complex digital transformation project portfolios. She spoke about her career in an organisation that she described as being psychologically safe. She was supported, she was encouraged and she loved to collaborate. She shared ideas openly and felt valued. She was motivated and performed at her peak when she was inspired by her peers. Later in this chapter, we talk about Susan's PCM, and what she did to ensure the confidence crisis didn't snowball.

✏️ Reflection point

From what you know of psychological safety, rate your current workplace environment on a scale of 1 to 10, with 10 being the best. Consider how safe you feel speaking up, sharing ideas, seeking and providing feedback and admitting when you don't know something. How comfortable are you in asking for help or speaking up when you've made a mistake? Do you feel safe collaborating, taking risks and experimenting in new ways of thinking? We'll build your awareness in these areas as we work through this chapter.

The signs of psychologically unsafe corporate environments

Some signs of psychologically unhealthy corporate environments include:

- toxic leadership – for example:
  - leaders who want to control every situation and decision
  - leaders who criticise people for any actions or issues
  - leaders who are interested in their own self-image and take all the glory and recognition for the work of others
- new ideas being shut down and collaboration not encouraged
- bullying and harassment, including:
  - harassing or offending
  - excluding people from decisions
  - keeping information from others
- organisational politics that are manipulative and self-serving
- workplace discrimination, including:
  - discrimination based on race, gender, sexuality or age
  - not fostering environments of inclusivity or diversity.

You've likely seen some – or perhaps even all – of these factors in a corporate environment you've worked in. It's important to also understand that some corporations have good workplace cultures and environments but the actual team that the individual is in can still be psychologically unsafe. In that instance, the environment comes down to the leader of that team, and the leadership style and culture that individual is cultivating in their team and in the team structure.

While workplace harassment continues to be a global issue, momentum for action is building because of the global MeToo movement. This has resulted in some high-profile cases, and action and accountability being taken. In Australia, the Australian Human Rights Commission produced its *Respect@Work: National Inquiry into Sexual Harassment in Australian Workplaces* report in 2020, which included 55 recommendations. The Australian government is committed to fully implementing all recommendations of the *Respect@Work* report. On a more individual level, to help you understand how to bring these issues to the boardroom and your workplace, Chief Executive Women (CEW), under the initiative Respect is Everyone's Business, and also The Australian Institute of Company Directors, have developed toolkits to help – find out more at respect.cew.org.au or aicd.com.au.

Taking stock of your corporate environment and the style of your leader can help you understand if the corporate environment and culture is aligned to your values. Our research tells us that these being misaligned can be a trigger for a PCM. Understanding this aspect of what you cannot control is important. Many of our executives told us they didn't realise this misalignment at the time of their PCM but, once they did, they could stop personalising the situation, and focus on controlling the way they reacted and responded, by putting in place coping strategies to avoid the loss of confidence snowball effect.

We cannot reiterate these points enough – recognising the early signs of psychologically unsafe corporate environments can enable coping strategies to be implemented more quickly. During a PCM, an important step is taking stock of the things that you can control. Your corporate environment is likely one in which you cannot control everything. Understanding that the environment is not psychologically safe – and realising in most instances this is not a reflection on you personally or within your control – is important. However, in cases where you believe you are being targeted – for example, bullying and harassment – your focus needs to be on building your resilience and your personal wellbeing as well as seeking the appropriate support to navigate a pathway to resolution.

Going back to Susan's story, unfortunately the psychologically safe environment she had been working in didn't last. A few years later, when most of her team moved offshore, a new leadership team was formed in Australia. The new team brought in changes and the organisation became more politically minded. Susan didn't feel safe in speaking up and she stopped sharing ideas. In meetings, her persona changed. Instead of being a confident, motivating and flourishing individual, she came across as nervous and hesitant – which stemmed from self-doubt – and this affected her performance. This was a PCM. It crippled her confidence and added weight to an emerging confidence snowball. Susan, finally recognising this moment for what it was, took action, engaged executive coaching support and changed jobs. She's now flourishing in her career again.

Remember – the early signs of a psychologically unsafe environment may not be obvious. As demonstrated in the preceding examples (and continuing through this chapter), you need to analyse early and identify what you are experiencing. This enables you to adopt coping strategies critical to preventing a declining confidence snowball taking hold.

✐ Reflection point

Now that you have learned more about psychologically unsafe environments and what they look like, reconsider the ratings you gave your workplace and adjust as required.

Navigating politics to boost confidence

No doubt you have seen or participated in some form of organisational politics. The female executives we spoke with told us they were often uncomfortable with incorporating political skills into their repertoire.

A white paper by the global Centre for Creative Leadership, 'Women and Political Savvy', discusses that many managers acknowledge that political savviness is an important skill to getting ahead, but still feel uncomfortable about it as they question the ethics of the behaviours they witness. Managers described the behaviours as 'inauthentic, manipulative and ultimately self-serving'. But what does it mean to be 'politically savvy'?

Identified as a key leadership competency in the Lominger Leadership Competency framework, political savvy is defined in the framework as follows:

> Can maneuver through complex political situations effectively and quietly; is sensitive to how people and organizations function; anticipates where the land mines are and plans his/her approach accordingly; views corporate politics as a necessary part of organizational life and works to adjust to that reality; is a maze-bright person.

Another interesting definition of political savviness comes from the Office of Human Resources in the United States:

> The ability to exhibit confidence and professional diplomacy while effectively relating to people at all levels, internally and externally. It demonstrates an understanding of the relationships and roles and responsibilities of your organisation.

This definition picks up on two key elements:

1. confidence (trust yourself!)
2. professional diplomacy (being sensitive and tactful in the process).

This is an interesting point of reflection, and shows political savviness is an important leadership competency. And, traditionally, these are

the kinds of skills – communicating strongly and making connections with others – that women excel at. So why did the women
we spoke with view being 'political' so negatively? Research more
widely points to it not just being women who view office politics
negatively – men do as well – but many women tend to view general political behaviour as self-serving and even, at times, akin to
bullying. In its more toxic form, it's unacceptable and manipulative.
When it's neither good nor bad and simply neutral, it can just be
part of organisational life. Rather than trying to avoid or ignore it,
politically savvy individuals can use their influence in an authentic
and sincere manner – and in such a way that all parties involved get
something positive out of the relationship.

The Center for Creative Leadership surveyed 334 participants
from its leadership development and women's leadership programs.
They found that those who are politically savvy have better career
prospects and career opportunities, and are seen as more promot-
able. In particular, the following behaviours seem to vary according
to political savviness and how an individual is politically turning up
within an organisation:

- the ability to build collaborative relationships
- the composure of an individual
- the ability for the individual to put people at ease and make
  them feel comfortable
- individual career management.

Despite all the positive information on organisational politics, it
seems that female executives are still less likely than male executives
to find themselves in situations where opportunity for promotion,
access to mentors and encouragement to take risks exist. These
unique barriers make it more critical than ever for women to embrace
and develop politically savvy skills.

Like it or not, developing political savviness is important as you navigate corporate environments. This is a necessary skill to get things done – especially when you need to influence outcomes that may not be in your direct control. Without this skill, you could become blindsided.

Marianne recalls a time she was left frustrated, when she was responsible for a division that serviced the needs of clients through a solution that was delivered in another business unit. To provide a better customer experience, her team needed some changes to the internal policies. Despite all efforts to work collaboratively with the leader of the other business unit, no traction could be made. Marianne and her team had strong working relationships and had engaged with the other team, educated them, and shared customer stories highlighting the importance of the required change. Both business unit teams agreed the change made sense; however, the leader of the other business unit was a blocker of the changes. It was a very frustrating 12 months. In the end, the reality of the situation was that the other business unit leader had no financial incentive to make the change, because any additional sales did not end up in their results. Interestingly, 12 months later, the business unit that Marianne was leading was transferred into the other leader's division. At that point, the changes were made. On reflection, the political play was obvious; the leader of the other business unit could see the growth potential.

Looking back, Marianne could see this was a situation of political manoeuvring – a very common scenario in business. When these types of situations occur in the workplace, obstacles are usually put up. In these situations it's important not to personalise the situation. At the time, Marianne thought it was her communication style, negotiation style or ability to influence, or that she hadn't provided enough facts to explain the situation. She spent more and more time preparing for every meeting, working through how to better cooperate, collaborate and communicate.

Marianne's efforts made no difference because the individual never spoke up about their intentions. Without transparency and consultation, they were working to transfer that part of the business. Once Marianne saw the situation for what it was she accepted that nothing she could have done would have changed the outcome. However, understanding this at the time could have reduced her stress.

✐ Reflection point

Rate your politically savvy skills on a scale of 1 to 10. Think about a situation or a problem at work. As you read through the following list, take note of where you rate yourself:

- Are you able to analyse the situation or context?
- Have you built the right partnerships and alliances to help you solve the problem?
- Can you keep conflict to a minimum?
- Do you have a strong reputation?

Women have the opportunity to reshape the future of work

A popular topic before the pandemic, psychological safety is now being discussed even more openly, given its relevance to agility, diversity and inclusion, and remote working. Quoted in the *McKinsey Quarterly* 2020 interview 'Psychological safety, emotional intelligence, and leadership in a time of flux', Professor Amy Edmondson argued,

As counterintuitive as it might seem, in many settings I'm seeing more psychological safety during the pandemic because of the greater collective fear about something very real – and, by the way, very external.

For many people during the pandemic, the explicit physical lack of safety has been experienced as a shared fear, which has allowed them to be more open and show vulnerabilities, and voice their thoughts and concerns with colleagues. This collective fear has become a potential driver of collaboration and innovation. It's contributing to a more open environment for producing and sharing ideas that, under normal conditions, may have remained unshared.

We must point out that we are covering people in corporate environments and the situation is different for our important essential workers – many of them continue to say they do not feel physically safe while they are required to show up to work. As a further complication, they may not be able to speak up because of the nature of their work.

As corporate environments move to hybrid models, we have an opportunity to redesign the corporate workplace to better foster psychological safety. Post-COVID-19, the great resignation and war for talent increased and we're now entering a time of economic challenges. Corporate cultures need to be built that will attract and retain people. These new ways of working – of inclusion, remote working, agility and more openness in communication – are environments where women tend to flourish. It's important that we take these learnings and continue to adapt them into the workplace and encourage them.

Further increased focus on emotional wellbeing and understanding of work–life balance and pressures has highlighted the importance of building workplaces and environments where executive women can be seen, make connections and thrive.

In January 2021, a report by CEMS Global Alliance in Management Education found leaders who build psychological safety will thrive post the COVID-19 pandemic. The report outlined findings from their survey of over 1700 managers, senior executives, board members and CEOs of large corporations from 34 countries. Of these respondents, 87 per cent said that COVID-19 had profoundly impacted businesses. While no consensus could be seen as to whether the impact was positive or negative, the report highlighted that the pandemic had

accelerated change in attitudes, expectations and mindsets; a shift from the rigid structure and systems that have long characterised organisations and models of leadership to something more flexible, open and agile.

The report concluded that leaders needed greater resilience and faster decision-making processes to ensure business longevity. The number one recommendation from the survey findings was that leaders must build psychologically safe environments for people to thrive in and work under modern-day pressures.

In the same interview with *McKinsey Quarterly*, Amy Edmondson also said, 'With tools like Zoom, communications have become more explicit and structured; leaders must ask direct questions about what's working and what isn't'.

Given the increased flexibility and opportunities for remote and hybrid work environments, it is important for leaders to create psychologically safe environments while also ensuring women are not disadvantaged. A *Harvard Business Review* article, 'Why WFH isn't necessarily good for women', states three key issues for leaders to consider before declaring working from home as an equaliser for women. These issues include:

- The work and family conflict can increase, given women are still more likely to take on more of the domestic responsibilities.
- Access to informal networks can reduce, suggesting not being seen or in the office can hinder any informal discussions.

- 'Presenteeism' can be rewarded, where only those who are in the office and 'in sight' of leaders are included in those informal, quick decision-making discussions.

While these aspects need to be considered, they should not hinder creating a workforce that allows women to thrive and gives them the flexibility needed – and, importantly, gives everyone a psychologically safe workplace. To combat these issues, the authors of 'Why WFH isn't necessarily good for women', suggest leaders need to ensure they turn to the facts and use evidence-based data to understand what roles and skillsets benefit from remote working. Leaders also need to understand the workplace culture and how the use of technology is affected, and take active steps to ensure any embedded assumptions about gender norms do not create any negative perceptions of those who take up remote working options. Importantly, organisations and leaders should focus on outputs not physical presence as a measure of peak performance.

✏ Reflection point

Review your ratings of how psychologically safe or unsafe your corporate environment is. Have any of those factors shifted with the new ways of working that have emerged post-COVID-19?

Summing up

Workplaces can kill your confidence. Psychological safety is the degree to how safe people perceive their corporate environments to be, with safer environments being those where they can share ideas and speak up. When workplaces are psychologically unsafe, they cripple confidence and can be a critical trigger for a PCM. Understanding this can help you recognise the early signs and the environmental issues that are out of your control. Political savviness is a critical skill to help you navigate the corporate environment. Working remotely has helped improve psychological safety in many workplaces. However, it's important to consider new workplace routines to ensure your key relationships continue to develop and communication is elevated intentionally to compensate for those unstructured interactions that no longer occur. You may need to more actively seek out career-enhancing opportunities. We need to make sure women do not become invisible.

Understand that psychologically unsafe environments are contributing to your loss of confidence and, if you stay in this situation, the lack of confidence and stress and anxiety will snowball. Evaluate your corporate environment and your responses to the tasks completed in this chapter. If you are experiencing an environment that is not psychologically safe, you may be moving towards – or already in – a PCM. If this isn't addressed, your confidence snowball may result in a career avalanche.

Your health and wellbeing are critically important for maintaining confidence during any PCM. The next chapter looks at how smart women end up in a situation where an erosion of confidence has knock-on effects into other areas of life. Even smart people burn out.

5

Your wellbeing underpins confidence

Take care of your body. It's the only place you have to live.
Jim Rohn

Your wellbeing forms the foundation for the resilience needed during a pivotal career moment (PCM). The absence of this foundation may trigger a lack of confidence snowball, which can turn into a career avalanche. Alternatively, a declining health situation may be the cause of a PCM. Either way, your wellbeing underpins your confidence throughout this journey.

What is wellbeing? According to the Oxford Dictionary, wellbeing is 'the state of being comfortable, healthy, or happy' – which are very broad and complex topics conveniently lumped together under the banner of wellbeing. Wellbeing is subjective. What 'comfortable' means to you or what makes you happy is your personal definition, and this may differ for others. But do you know what your definition is and the important actions required to gain or maintain this state? That is what we help you define in this chapter.

The amazing and highly educated executive women we met in our research knew that wellbeing was important, and yet they struggled to maintain it and even experienced burnout during various stages of their career. Some even had executive health checks provided by their organisation and still didn't take up this opportunity because they were too busy. In this chapter, we explore why this kind of access to knowledge and care is ignored, the risk this can create for confidence levels and career, and the importance of self-compassion. Many people – women included – are reluctant to discuss the nuances that make women different from men. Female-specific health, medical treatments and biological cycles can be taboo subjects, especially in the workplace. Our research indicates a level of discomfort for certain conversations, particularly those around perimenopause and menopause. In our experience, women don't do themselves any favours by taking on a 'nothing to see here' mindset to women's health. Many fear that acknowledging these differences reignites a negative narrative around women's reliability and capability in the workforce. Some women we spoke with even asked us not to discuss this in our book, saying, 'You are taking us back decades'. In this chapter, we want to normalise this conversation and acknowledge the physical and mental wellbeing issues that often accompany or even cause women's PCMs.

Our research showed that the concept of self-compassion is also not widely discussed or accepted as a strategy by executive women. We dive into this further in this chapter, and identify the connection between self-compassion and self-esteem.

Physical and mental wellbeing is equally important in managing confidence. As mentioned, PCMs can be brought on by women's health issues. Some of our executive women reflected back that during times of – in some cases, serious – health concerns, warning signs were ignored. The dots between the physical and mental impacts on women's health and confidence in career performance were not connected. They soldiered on, aiming towards high expectations. As they faltered, however, the lack of confidence snowballed. Instead of the confidence-building that can come from care, nurturing and understanding of self, stress, anxiety and fear took hold, further compounding the snowball effect.

Balancing wellbeing

It's a 'chicken and egg' situation – and while it doesn't really matter which one comes first, we do know that confidence builds wellbeing and wellbeing builds confidence. The confidence and stress snowball for some of the executive women we interviewed also indicated a shift away from a focus on wellbeing. This focus on wellbeing is exactly what's needed to build resilience and confidence. Wellbeing is foundational to maintain stability during turbulent times such as a PCM.

An example of this is our interviewee Sally, an entrepreneur, business owner and author across financial services and media, who we introduced you to in chapter 2. Sally described how during a time of incredible stress in her business – her hands were shaking while she was driving and her anxiety was so high she needed medication. Her health was going downhill; however, her mindset was to push through. Eventually, the symptoms and medical advice were a wake-up call. She knew things had to change. As a person who lives on the edge – a risk-taker and an entrepreneur – she now finds solace in focusing on her family and taking some time out for herself. (Sally does her thinking in the bath, with her family often joking that she's in the bath every day.) Sally demonstrates grit and tenacity through finding ways to keep her cup full and filling it quickly. However, she recognises the need to bring a more holistic approach to her wellbeing is a constant challenge.

Susan, who we also introduced in chapter 2 (a strategic C-suite executive experienced in global technology), also highlighted the connection between wellbeing and confidence. In her interview with us, she recognised that when she's not sleeping well or enough, when she's not exercising, when things aren't in balance with her family, the negative self-talk starts. This immediately affects her confidence.

Physical and mental wellbeing are each equally important to managing confidence throughout your career journey. Some defined elements around wellbeing have been around for decades. When you think about general wellbeing, for example, you might recall Maslow's hierarchy of needs. This hierarchy is displayed as a triangle, based on the idea that we build from a foundational level of basic physiological needs (food, water, warmth and rest), and then fulfil other needs. What we would like to explore with you is the notion that all the elements that influence wellbeing are important and all have equal footing in terms of their impact. As outlined in figure 2, we've taken what we see as the eight most important wellbeing elements and split them into internal and external elements to create the Wellbeing Wheel.

Figure 2: Internal and external elements of the Wellbeing Wheel

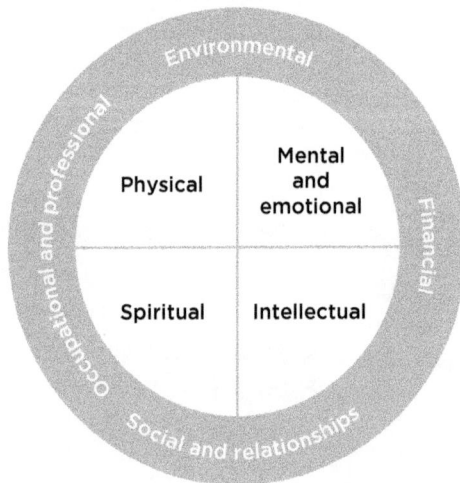

First, let's look at the internal elements that affect your wellbeing, and the components within each one. These are:

- Physical:
  - exercise
  - diet
  - sleep
  - interacting with nature, hobbies
  - your daily activities, routines and positive habits.
- Mental and emotional:
  - being in tune with yourself
  - your ability to cope with the challenges and emotional ups and downs of life
  - the resilience that you build and tap into as learning
  - your mindset.
- Spiritual:
  - your faith and religious beliefs
  - your source of peace and harmony
  - your purpose and meaning
  - values that provide your vision and direction.
- Intellectual:
  - ability to remain curious
  - learning and growing
  - being open to new ideas and agile thinking
  - creativity and innovation
  - enjoying the journey of discovery not just the destination.

The external elements that influence your wellbeing, and the sub-elements within them, are as follows:

- Environmental:
  - the quality of your environments to help you thrive

- the safety, support and security of those environments to help you feel safe.

- Financial:
  - being able to live comfortably and plan for the future.

- Social and relationships:
  - how you relate and connect with people
  - the quality and supportiveness of relationships.

- Occupational and professional:
  - the fulfilment that you gain from your job, regardless of what that job is
  - the ability or the sense of contribution and value-adding
  - feeling of mastery and expertise
  - shared learning, coaching and mentoring.

All these elements are related to your wellbeing and, therefore, boost your resilience to bounce back from confidence challenges. Decreased attention to any element of wellbeing will cause a dented or unbalanced wheel. It may still go around, but the journey is getting rougher. Many executive women don't realise their wellbeing is not in balance until it's too late. The impacts of this may vary – for some areas, an immediate affect can be felt; for other areas, as with a slow leak in a tyre, the full impact may not at first be noticed, but can take hold when we least expect it. Either way, these wellbeing impacts all contribute to the lack of confidence snowball and career avalanche.

Focusing on wellbeing is often seen as theoretical – put in the 'should do' category or tacked onto the end of the 'to-do list' but not prioritised. Women executives often feel overwhelmed by the scale of this task of wellbeing. Our successful executive women tended to be 'Type A' personalities. These personality types like to set big goals, but taking even small steps towards your wellbeing factors can have a positive impact. You don't have to make your wellbeing a full-time job. Setting realistic goals around wellbeing can enable sustainable change. Both of us love running and like to train for set events. Marianne set as her fitness goal completing her second international marathon, while Vanessa was training for her first half marathon. We both achieved the event goals we set out to achieve. But once initial goals such as these are achieved, general wellbeing goals need to be reassessed. Big goals can be motivating when everything lines up well for a specific event, but post-event, we both struggled to maintain that same level of fitness. It wasn't sustainable and this impacted our motivation. When it comes to general health and wellbeing, slow and steady steps that create small habits are more effective than boom and bust goals.

A PCM can happen at any time and if you don't prioritise your own wellbeing, you reduce your resiliency – in other words, your ability to deal with uncertainty and change and your ability to bounce back from adversity. This puts your confidence at risk. Perhaps you're thinking, *I exercise regularly and eat well.* Indeed, our interviewees also described focusing on being in better physical shape. If you wake up feeling physically strong and fit, you're in a better position to be confident, competent and able to manage stress. The women we interviewed believe that physical fitness levels are linked to your mental wellbeing. But remember that all the other elements of your wellbeing wheel also need to be in balance and attended to.

We know that mental health concerns have exploded in the wake of COVID-19. This is serious. Attending to both internal and external wellbeing is key to mental wellbeing. Simple and evidence-based techniques to boost mental wellbeing and resilience include practices such as mindfulness and meditation, a gratitude journal (writing three things you are grateful for every day), random acts of kindness to others, immersing yourself in nature (such as a forest walk or a swim in the ocean), connecting with others and finding joy (this might be via a lavender bath with candles or a family games night, doing a puzzle or watching a TED Talk). As a personal example, Vanessa finds joy singing with the Hummingsong women's choir every Monday night.

If you or anyone you know is struggling with mental health, please reach out or encourage others to seek professional help. This cannot be overstated.

Amelia, introduced in part I, experienced this firsthand when she was diagnosed with breast cancer. She said her focus on well-being, including regular swimming and walking, contributed to a solid fitness level, both physically and mentally. Her medical team commented she was in a strong position for her treatment and her fight with breast cancer. Our observation was that Amelia drew upon all elements of the wellbeing wheel.

Constant rebalancing across internal and external wellbeing elements is important so you don't form a flat spot in your wellbeing wheel.

✎ **Reflection point**

Table 2 lists the eight wellbeing elements outlined in this section. Note down your own personal stocktake of your current level of wellbeing in each area. And, against each of the factors, write down one small habit you could introduce or change that would move you along to your desired level. Of course, check with your health professional before making any changes.

Table 2: Eight wellbeing elements

Wellbeing elements	Your stocktake assessment: Current level, scale of 1 (low) to 5 (high)	One tiny habit you could introduce or change
Physical		
Mental and emotional		
Spiritual		
Intellectual		
Environmental		
Financial		
Social and relationships		
Occupational and professional		

Women's health – the conversations female executives don't have

Few people, male or female, like talking about women's health issues at work. Many women don't recognise physical symptoms that can affect their confidence, and this is particularly the case with peri-menopause and menopause. This lack of understanding and silence has an impact on women, especially when it comes to accessing support about women's health. How do we move beyond the fear that women will be perceived as unreliable, moody beings in the grip of hormones? Women have worked hard to dispel these myths for decades. However, silence is not sustainable.

In our research, 64.6 per cent of the executive women we surveyed had experienced perimenopausal or menopausal symptoms, with 24.6 per cent stating these symptoms had a significant impact on their ability to function optimally in their role. This is a significant issue for women. The average age for menopause in Australia is 51, but perimenopausal symptoms can start five to 10 years before your last period. Of the executive women that we surveyed, the majority were between 45 and 55 years old, with 30 per cent being between 55 and 64. Executive women are often at the peak of their careers when these changes to their health and wellbeing are having such a big impact.

In our survey, 52.8 per cent of responses, from both women and men, identified as not being comfortable in discussing the symptoms of perimenopause in the work environment, with a further 17.6 per cent picking the not sure/sitting on the fence response. This makes a total of 70.4 per cent of respondents who are not committing to being comfortable with this conversation. A lack of conversation further contributes to women's health topics being taboo. This negatively impacts women – not because of perpetuating myths, but because of the lonely struggle.

Women don't often get the support or medical advice they need during this time. For some women, the symptoms of perimenopause are not obvious and are more generalised. Women may stop feeling like themselves during this time. Something just isn't right. Exactly what is wrong can be difficult to determine, but these more generalised symptoms can lead to an unsettling period. Other symptoms might raise concerns of more dire health conditions. Oprah Winfrey has described how she worried about heart palpitations and sleeplessness for two years – and consulted her doctor and cardiologist – before discovering these were signs of perimenopause. With no conversation, women can worry.

Respected GP Dr Edwina shared that most women she sees do not understand what the symptoms of perimenopause are, mainly because they're not widely discussed.

Over the course of writing this book, it's been great to see this topic being discussed more. Leaders such as ANZ New Zealand's CEO Antonia Watson are sharing their experiences – as Antonia states, 'to remove that stigma attached to menopause and ensure it is not a barrier to success'. Further, and for the first time, women's health issues such as menopause were discussed in the 2022 Australian federal budget as a barrier to workplace participation, although no budget to address the issue was allocated.

Kylie was a well-respected change leader and project director in a complex global transport business. Her early menopause was the perfect storm with her PCM and she had no idea. When Vanessa first met Kylie, she was distressed, feeling the despair of losing her connection with the confident, capable person she used to be. She felt lost and self-critical, and couldn't figure out her own pathway through her PCM. During a coaching conversation, Vanessa recognised the symptoms of perimenopause from her own experience. Kylie hadn't considered what she was feeling could be connected to her body going through early menopause due to surgery. Fortunately, Kylie sought medical support and she was able to put the right treatments in place, which enabled her to stabilise her symptoms and rebuild her confidence. She rebuilt her resilience, navigated her way through this challenging PCM, and is now a successful consultant specialising in organisational change and transformation, as well as being a non-executive director and kicking some amazing personal goals.

Vanessa empathised with Kylie based on her own personal story with perimenopause in her 40s – during which she was also unsure of what was happening and experiencing confidence-crippling symptoms she wasn't expecting. It took years before she finally had the right conversation with health practitioners to get her the support she needed to find her old self again.

This is an important conversation women need to have. If we are to normalise these experiences, executive women need to lead by example, being brave and encouraging dialogue. Men also have an important role to play in better understanding these issues, and showing a willingness to encourage dialogue. If we truly believe in creating diverse, inclusive, psychologically safe environments, women need to feel comfortable to raise, discuss and find the support needed for all aspects of their health and wellbeing. It was encouraging to read columnist Jacqueline Maley's article 'Why older women dare not mention the M word' in *Sydney Morning Herald*, where she reported,

> On September 29 [2021], Australia's Chief Scientist, Dr Cathy Foley, gave a speech to the Institute of Public Administration Australia where she didn't just mention the M word – menopause – she focused on it.

Maley went on to discuss the recent research from Britain that indicates around a million women in Britain have left their jobs as a result of menopause symptoms – right at a time when women should be embracing their seniority as well as being role models for younger women in the workplace. Women are reluctant to talk to managers about symptoms for fear of damaging their career or being ridiculed. 'We can be sure these same things are happening in Australia, and women are leaving work because of it,' Maley quoted Foley as concluding.

Most women are aware of 'hot flushes' or 'hot flashes' as being part of perimenopause symptoms; however, many other, and at times unexpected, symptoms and flow-on impacts can throw women off kilter. To delve into this further, *The Feel Good Guide to Menopause* by Dr Nicola Gates is an informative read.

✎ Reflection point

Take the time to do a self-assessment. Where are you at? Are you not feeling like yourself? Are you experiencing any symptoms that could indicate perimenopause? Go to your GP and have a blood test to see what's happening. The important thing is to start the conversation. It might feel a little awkward, but by sharing experiences and talking with other executive women, you can start action to improve your wellbeing - and be part of creating an environment that enables women to thrive in their executive careers instead of leaving careers early, opting for lower positions or continuing to suffer in silence.

Recognising early PCM warning signs that are affecting your wellbeing

So far we have discussed PCMs and what they look like. Now let's talk about some of the typical impacts PCMs can have on your wellbeing. By detecting the early warning signs and thinking about what you're experiencing and how you're responding, you can recognise a PCM in its early stages.

Our research indicates the following signs that confidence is on the decline:

- negative self-talk
- being overly self-critical
- nervousness
- anxiety
- stress
- not sleeping
- exhaustion
- procrastination
- uncertainty
- withdrawal and isolation
- burying yourself in work
- not adopting a growth mindset
- having a fixed mindset where you can't progress beyond where you are
- spending time focusing outside of your circle of control.

Under stress, our brains move into a fight, flight or freeze response. Our brains naturally use this response to protect us against threats. When registering stress, our brain plays a role in prediction, anticipating the worst so we can be prepared. It will naturally err on the side of caution because we are biologically wired to keep ourselves safe. Sometimes, however, this stress response can cause you to catastrophise if you're not careful. If you don't care for your physical, mental and emotional wellbeing, and nurture yourself and be kind to yourself, you can risk spiralling into a lack of confidence snowball. We talk about self-compassion in a moment; however, recognising the early signs and intervening quickly can help prevent a career avalanche.

Our interviewee Grace's executive career was in the wealth management industry. She has worked for large, listed companies and is now founder and CEO of a start-up technology company. When Grace's confidence started to drop, she noticed that if anyone started to question her or her direction, she would typically go into an attack mode – a type of fight or flight response – rather than a self-reflection mode where she was tapping into more rational thinking.

She used a coach to help her identify some of the triggers that sent her down this path. She hadn't previously noticed the physical manifestations and changes in demeanour when her confidence declined, and when this decline was gaining momentum. Getting in touch with those automatic responses and understanding and feeling the tension and stress in her body enabled her to put into place some strategies to calm this response. For example, she talked with us about meditation, simple breathing exercises that would help her and a long walk in nature, which she always found brought perspective.

In the award-winning book *Phosphorescence*, journalist Dr Julia Baird reinforces the importance of nature and the impact on our psychological and physiological sense of wellbeing when all of our senses are exposed to nature. She talks about research and evidence that indicates this practice of being in nature promotes wellbeing. Both of us know that when we run near the beach, we get that feeling of appreciation and enjoyment from being close to the majestic ocean. It's interesting to see our personal experience backed by research. Of course, this connection to land, sea and community is founded by the longest standing community in Australia – our First Nations peoples – who see connection to Country as an important part of rejuvenation.

> ✏️ **Reflection point**
>
> Now, take a moment to relax and, closing your eyes if needed, do a body scan. What are you noticing about yourself? Are any early warning signs of PCM starting to show? Where are your shoulders sitting? What are your typical stress indicators and how do you rate them on a scale of 'calm', 'tense' or 'distress'? How are you reacting and responding to family, friends and colleagues? What is the narrative going on in your mind? What's the chatter that you're listening to? Reflect on positive and effective habits you may have started.

Challenge old thinking around self-compassion

Old thinking around self-compassion tends to focus on selfishness and being self-centred or narcissistic. But self-compassion is treating yourself with the same kindness, care and concern that you would show a loved one. Dr Kristin Neff discusses this in *Self-Compassion: The Proven Power of Being Kind to Yourself*, where she looks at self-kindness versus self-judgement, common humanity versus being in isolation, and mindfulness versus over-identification. Self-compassion needs to balance out self-esteem. (We will explore the differences between self-esteem and self-compassion in a moment.)

Dr Neff goes on to break this into tender self-compassion and fierce self-compassion. We need to combine fierceness with tenderness. Tenderness is about being kind to ourselves by being reassuring and present with our situation. Fierceness is about standing tall – to protect ourselves, draw those boundaries and do things differently if we are in negative situations. Our survey asked participants to identify strategies they used during confidence loss. Self-compassion was identified by only 24 per cent of respondents. With a better understanding of self-compassion, it can become embedded as a life tool and not just a strategy to turn to at times of stress.

Links also exist between self-compassion and a growth mindset – the belief that change, learning and growth is possible.

Let's explore the concept of a growth mindset before we move on. Carol Dweck, a psychology professor at Stanford University, has spent decades researching and writing about the benefits of adopting what she called a 'growth mindset'. As opposed to a 'fixed mindset', where we believe our personality and ability will never change, a growth mindset is recognised in people who have a belief in their potential to learn, improve and grow. They ground themselves in a positive and optimistic belief that they can change their course with applied effort.

A fascinating *Harvard Business Review* article, 'Give yourself a break: The power of self-compassion' by Serena Chen – a professor of psychology at the University of California, Berkley – overlays further research combining these concepts. Chen discovered a direct correlation between self-compassion and a growth mindset – in fact, Chen's research suggests that self-compassion triggers people to adopt a growth mindset. One study in particular identified that self-compassion paved the way for self-improvement by revving up people's desire to do better, encouraging the belief that improvement is possible, and increasing motivation and drive.

There is a difference between self-compassion and self-esteem. High self-esteem can give you a sense of self-confidence and self-assuredness, but it can have its drawbacks. Without an acceptance that we are fabulously flawed human beings, continuously learning and growing, self-assuredness may miss those opportunities for learning. It may be fake confidence. The 'fake it till you make it' philosophy can shift us from inaction to action. This sense of momentum can build energy and can improve confidence. But fake confidence is a facade. It is inauthentic, which isn't a successful or sustainable strategy. Its fragility can lead to disastrous confidence snowball outcomes. On the other end of the spectrum, self-criticism causes performance anxiety, stress and procrastination, which also prevents you from learning from mistakes and causes you to miss opportunities. This is not conducive to building resilience for your PCM and your executive career progression.

Hiding behind an inauthentic facade may look great on the surface, but executives we've worked with found this difficult to maintain. Self-compassion, however, prevents negative emotions from taking over and allows you to tap into a more accurate assessment of the situation, as well as the motivation to learn and grow from the circumstances.

Three executives we interviewed stood out in particular in this area. Bernadette is an entrepreneur and business owner, growing a business that was acquired by a global leader in the people solutions space. Bernadette, along with Eliza and Amelia (both introduced in part I), all demonstrated self-compassion in their interviews.

Bernadette advocates self-compassion and an overall focus on the balance of wellbeing. She is a leader and future of work and wellbeing advocate who actively promotes and demonstrates workplace gender equality, diversity and inclusion along with balance and wellbeing. Bernadette talks about and demonstrates the importance of fitting our own oxygen mask first. She describes confidence as a belief in yourself and an innate positivity. This enables her to reframe her setbacks, both personally and professionally, be kind to herself, identify learnings and move on.

Eliza, in a PCM, assessed that the environment wasn't conducive for her wellbeing. She chose self-compassion and authenticity, enabling her to approach her exit from the organisation with openness. Personal growth moments happened, which she described with great appreciation, during what could be seen by some as a time to keep your head down and flee. Once Eliza focused on self-compassion and holistic wellbeing, her lack of confidence snowball slowed and was eventually busted. Despite the circumstances, her six-month exit plan was successfully completed and she transitioned immediately into a dream executive role she loves.

Amelia talked about how learning to approach her career with self-compassion enabled her to take a smoother, calmer and more curious approach to some challenging times. She adopted this approach to learning and growth across her professional career, and more recently when battling a different type of PCM with breast cancer. Self-compassion is a way to build a balanced wellbeing foundation. Amelia is truly inspirational.

⌀ Reflection point

To further reflect on your self-compassion, in 'Give yourself a break: The power of self-compassion' Serena Chen suggests using the following three-point checklist:

1. Am I being kind and understanding to myself?
2. Do I acknowledge shortcomings and failure as experiences shared by everyone?
3. Am I keeping my negative feelings in perspective?

Reflect on a PCM you have already experienced (or are experiencing), or times when a confidence crisis has started to snowball for you. What can you learn that can assist with your ongoing personal journey to self-compassion? How can you be ready for the next PCM?

Summing up

Wellness is more than a cliché heading. It needs to be unpacked and broken down into its eight component parts – the internal and external factors we've outlined in this chapter. Your wellbeing is foundational for building resilience, preventing the confidence crisis snowball and mitigating a career avalanche. Early warning signs your wellbeing is not prioritised include change of energy, poor sleep, tension, stress, anxiety, withdrawal, isolation, burying yourself in work, procrastination and avoidance, and change in eating habits (such as reaching more often for the biscuit barrel or lolly jar or having that extra coffee). These signs are not confidence building; they are stress indicators that can lead to a confidence snowball.

Many executive women are feeling the impact of perimenopausal symptoms but are not comfortable having a conversation about it. Seeking information, conversation and support from others – and, importantly, professional advice – will help you through this journey. Self-compassion will build your confidence by tapping into your willingness to be kind to yourself, to accept that there is room to grow and explore with a growth mindset, and to stand up and set boundaries for yourself.

Challenge your thinking. Bring self-compassion to the top of your agenda. Stop thinking that a successful executive needs to be highly critical, focused on performance at all costs or take a 'suck it up and get on with it' approach. Stop the negative narrative and change this to a constructive growth and learning opportunity. We've seen through our research that when you apply this kind of mindset, belief and attitude, you slow down and can even bust your confidence snowball. Instead of criticising and chastising yourself, be kinder to yourself. The research shows you will perform better.

Doing this alone is not the best strategy for your confidence, especially when experiencing a PCM – and you don't have to. Our next chapter delves into the importance of your support crew during a PCM. We cover how to build one and how to effectively tap into one, and how your support crew can be of best value during a PCM – when your confidence decline may be about to happen.

6

The role of your support crew

I learnt a long time ago the wisest thing I can do is be on my own
side, be an advocate for myself and others like me.
Maya Angelou

In the two previous chapters, we covered the role your workplace environment and your wellbeing play in either contributing to your pivotal career moment (PCM) or helping you navigate through it. The third and final factor we want to cover in this part is the role of your support crew.

During a PCM, the quality and diversity of your support crew critically impacts your ability to bounce back from that moment, regain confidence and continue your successful path. Our research and experience tells us that when executives were in a PCM, the support provided by their support crew was one of the key strategies that helped them navigate away from the crisis of confidence snowball effect.

It's important to build your crew as soon as you start your career. If you don't have a crew, this chapter provides some tips to help you to start building and thinking about your support network. If you have a crew, we also cover how you can engage with them during your PCM, and make sure that you have the right crew for any future PCMs.

Your support crew needs to be a group with diverse skills, different lived experiences and different backgrounds – for example, different cultural backgrounds, ages and industry experiences. The more diverse the group, the more enriched the feedback and support you will receive.

But there is a limit to the advice in this chapter. The PCMs we're talking about are circumstances that impact your career and result in stress and anxiety, but don't put you at risk in terms of dire health or mental wellbeing. In the latter situations, it is important to seek professional help beyond your crew. If you're in doubt and you know that your wellbeing is affected in these moments, you must contact your GP and they can get you started with a medical assessment.

In this chapter, we're going to talk about understanding the support you need, building your crew, and how going it alone or in isolation only snowballs the lack of confidence, increases that negative self-talk and may even encourage ego and shame. Our interviewees all discussed the importance of their support crew during their PCM. It was one of the contributing factors to successfully navigating through the PCM and regaining their confidence. It's important to understand that you may have different support crews for different times. Identify the crew members who are right for you, at the right time.

What is a support crew?

Your support crew membership may change over your career, but what your crew represents will remain the same. Your crew is the people around you supporting you, who you know and trust. They have your best interests at heart. They are people who you choose and they are going to stay objective. They're going to respectfully challenge your ideas and decisions to make sure you are doing the right thing for yourself. They are people who will and can support you and allow you to be your true self. They will have no judgements, even if you need to let off some steam or ask any questions.

We're not talking about the colleagues in your team. These are important people who you may collaborate with and work with to suit the needs of your organisation. What we're talking about for your crew is people who are focused on your needs. We're also not talking about broader networks. These broader networks are important groups of people you'll have throughout your career. These networks are wide and large, and include people you will engage with at certain times during the course of your career.

Your crew is a small group of people who will provide support to you at various times. They need to be people you can trust because you may have to share with them sensitive or confidential information. Your crew can include your family and friends, and may need to provide a range of support during a PCM. But you also need people who can challenge your views and provide you with some objectivity and perspective on the situation.

Understanding what a support crew is – and what it isn't – can help ensure you don't invite advice from the wrong people. You can also look at the current crew that you have and think about any changes you need, to make sure you're getting the right advice that will support you at that time.

Your crew members need to be trustworthy. Your crew might not be the people who share the same interests, opinions and views as you; instead, they might challenge you, while still caring about you. Some have people in their crew who have totally opposite views. The more diverse your crew, the better it is for you. It will give you that broad range of views and perspectives. It may not seem obvious at first, but your crew will contribute positively to your happiness and wellbeing.

You may not turn to everybody in your crew for every issue, but knowing the support you need helps you build the specific roles for each member, so you know who to turn to when you need a certain type of support.

Having loyal, trusted and caring people around you to turn to for support in a PCM will help you not only keep an objective view of what's happening around you, but also think more clearly about what's happening and avoid listening to that negative self-talk. You're more able to avoid that lack of confidence snowball and so continue to have a successful career.

Marianne recognised the need for a crew early on in her career. At the beginning as she was learning, her crew was initially people she could access information from, and collaborate and discuss issues with. The crew membership changed over time as she started to meet and connect with different people throughout her career and move up the career ladder. This crew provided a safe environment and challenged her views on issues, while also helping her navigate from finding problems to finding solutions.

In her early 30s, Marianne had an opportunity to lead an ASX-listed company. Whether she would take up the opportunity was a big decision at the time. Like many people – particularly women – imposter syndrome kicked in and Marianne focused on the aspects of the role she didn't have experience on. She reached out to a specific person in her crew, a retired CEO of a large company. He was 40 years Marianne's senior, and she selected him based on his lived experience over his long career. She wanted to understand his reflections and how he approached his CEO appointments. She asked questions to understand the contributing factors for his success. The reassuring feedback was that at the time of any appointment – female or male – no-one ever ticks all the boxes of the job requirements. Rather, they bring their own unique skills and have areas to grow into. It was as much about building a great team to fill those gaps as it was about her ability in the role. Other members of her crew also helped her negotiate the terms of the appointment and helped build her development plan. Marianne also engaged a professional coach, and that coach continues to remain a pivotal person in her crew.

As her needs over her career changed, Marianne has always had someone to reach out to. Marianne assembled the right crew members, who were able to provide the right support. They provided objectivity, opinions and views to understand the opportunity, and also identify her strengths and the skills she needed to develop. She would not have taken the opportunity if it wasn't for the support of her crew. On taking the opportunity, she became the youngest female CEO of an ASX-listed company. This inspired other women to take on senior roles.

✎ Reflection point

Think about the areas where you need support – either generally, or during your PCM. Identifying these areas is the first step to building your crew, but doing so can also help you check that you've got the right current crew members – people who can perform a support role for you in the areas you need. Write down in your journal the main areas you need support in.

Working out who should be in your crew

You need people in various categories and with various levels of intimacy in your crew. You should have at least the following types of support in your crew:

- *Emotional support:* These people listen and provide the love and support you need, with the positive pep talks or supportive actions that boost your overall morale and confidence.
- *Mental mind shifters:* These people help challenge your views and help you move from a fixed to a growth mindset. They are

likely to know or understand the environment and industry you operate in.

- *Financial knowledge support:* These people help you understand your value and the value you bring to any organisation. They may provide remuneration benchmarks and also help you negotiate any terms or conditions.
- *Career development support:* These people help with your goal setting and understand how to help you navigate the path to get to your desired state. This can be through a formal arrangement with a professional coach or someone with people and culture experience and skills.

Again, the more diverse your crew, the better. A diverse crew brings a variety of perspectives. It increases creativity and helps you to solve problems and find solutions faster.

The number of people in your crew can vary. Remember, it's not about the broader network that you have. It's about the smaller trusted group of five to 10 people. In the categories just outlined, you might have one or more people and, at certain times, you might need one or more people talking to you about the specific issues that you're facing in your PCM.

Have a look at who you think should be included across those different categories. Think about family and friends. They're often fantastic in the emotional support category and they might also provide some financial support. You'll likely have some professional connections, and some professional health support. Also consider your connections through any networks or associations you are part of – for example, professional associations linked to your career such as CPA Australia or Chartered Accountants Australia and New Zealand, law councils, medical associations. Think about broader associations such as the Australian Institute of Company Directors (AICD), Chief Executive Women (CEW), Women in Super and

Women in Media (we have provided a longer list in chapter 11). You may include your executive coach or similar professionals to help you bring perspective, models and frameworks to challenge and encourage you to think beyond your PCM.

Having the right people in your crew will help you navigate your PCM quicker. The evidence from our research indicated that people who had strong support crews were more objective in their thinking, and had new perspectives, an increased profile and brand, and better access to lots of different opportunities.

Your crew can also help you avoid that lack of confidence snowball and make sure that you get the support you need over your career. You'll know how to draw the right people into specific experiences, such as a PCM.

Remember – for most circumstances in your PCM, you will make it through either with your crew and/or with your executive coach. Again we reiterate, seek professional medical advice and support as required.

We understand that it is hard to draw on people for support, but try to have various people supporting you. People feel honoured when you reach out and ask for their help.

Marianne recently received the following note from a business connection:

Dear Marianne,

I've become aware of the need to surround myself with some supportive people. In the past, you've played a supportive role for me when it came to strategic insights into my career. I was wondering if you could provide that support for me now to help me navigate a current challenging career moment.

I'd also really like to know how I can reciprocate and help you.

Thank you.

When Marianne received this note, she immediately prioritised this catch-up – because she knew the courage it would have taken to share this situation and request help. The person was someone Marianne knew and respected, and she knew if they were reaching out it must have been for something important. Acts of service and kindness that support others also activate feel-good neurochemicals. So don't underestimate how important supporting you feels to your crew.

✎ Reflection point

Think about the areas of support you listed earlier in this chapter. If you have a support crew, do they have the right skills to provide you with support in these areas? If you don't have a support crew or need to fill certain areas, who could be in your crew to support you right now?

How engaging your crew will directly impact your confidence

When you're in a PCM, your thoughts and emotions can be impacted with negative self-talk creeping in. Your crew will help you navigate this moment, but also make sure that you avoid the lack of confidence snowball.

Over 60 per cent of our survey respondents told us that, at times when they lacked confidence, it was their crew who helped them through. An example of this is Audrey, from part I. Audrey had existing flexible work arrangements negotiated with her boss at the time. When a new boss took over the division she worked in, they kept questioning her existing flexible work arrangements. The agreement she had with the organisation was being disregarded and she was being invited to meetings at times when she had other commitments. This made Audrey feel helpless and guilty that she had these arrangements. She ended up trying to juggle a number of things. As a result, her performance was affected, as was her life and family. It was her support crew who helped her look at the situation objectively, and gave her the support and courage to speak to her boss to find out what the real issue was with her arrangements.

After this discussion, it became clear Audrey's boss hadn't understood the responsibilities that Audrey had, and they ended up in a great situation where he not only supported Audrey and encouraged her to continue with the flexible arrangements, but also used this as a great advocacy story in the company.

Over your work life, you'll have different crews for different times, and access different crew members at different times. But the composition of your crew should always be carefully considered. What is your crew make-up now? Is it right for you? You need to be able to engage with your crew when you need them, and be able to articulate what you are going through or feeling so that the person you've reached out to will know exactly how to give you the advice and support you need.

If you're in the situation where you need to reach out and start sharing about your current situation or triggers of your PCM, this can leave you open to dealing with vulnerabilities and even at worst shame. Take guidance from your crew – listen to their views and their support. If you have the right crew, you have the support to face your PCM and take action. Some of your crew will provide comfort and support, while others will provide practical advice such as for those tactical situations where you need to assemble people in each of the areas that you might need help, either now or sometime in the future. You can't lean on your emotional support crew if you need financial or technical skills. Certain people in your crew will only give you advice for skill development, while others are the right people for emotional support. Having the right people, knowing their role and knowing what support they'll provide will be critical for you to navigate that PCM.

Grace, from the previous chapter, shared a great example here. After a restructure, she found herself in a PCM. For the first time in her 30-year career, her role was made redundant and negative self-talk crept in. Her confidence was hit hard and her behaviour changed at work as well as at home. She felt isolated and ashamed. Three people in her crew noticed these changes in her behaviour – her husband, who was helping from an emotional support perspective, a colleague at work and a person in her professional peer network. They listened and provided her with support. On their advice, she sought out an executive career coach. This coach gave her frameworks to identify her skills and strengths and uncover opportunities where she could apply these, realigning with her passion, values and purpose. As a result, Grace ended up starting her own business. She has recently launched a product in a fintech company and she's never been happier.

✏ Reflection point

Think about your support crew: do you have all the areas of expertise and diversity of skills for the support you need? If not, think about who you can add or who can help you make new connections.

Schedule time to connect with your crew and contact them. Depending on the relationship that you have with them, this could be a phone call or an email.

A possible script could be:

> Dear [name],
>
> I'm not sure if you're aware that, following a company restructure, my role was changed/made redundant/ moved offshore. The impact of this event has rocked my confidence/made me rethink my career path, and I'd really appreciate your expert advice to help me navigate the situation. I would appreciate 30 minutes of your time in the next week or so and welcome your thoughts and insights on what my next steps could be. I can't tell you how thankful I am to have you in my support crew. I really look forward to talking with you. Just thinking about this has already helped me keep calm and focus on my future.
>
> Thank you.

Summing up

Your crew harbours an environment of safety, caring and compassion, as well as practical skills. They'll challenge your views and help you see multiple perspectives while having your best interests at heart. Executives with the right crews have successfully navigated their PCMs and continue to have successful careers.

Make sure you have the right people in your crew and that you are not surrounding yourself with people who don't have your best interests at heart. If they are not the right people, reflect on the role they did play. How can you replace them with the people you need right now for the issue that you're facing? Start to engage with your crew and get the right outcome for your PCM.

You are now armed with the knowledge of the support you need to get in place and how to utilise this to help you navigate through your PCM. Let's start to put all of these strategies together and create the path for you to continue your success.

The chapters in the next part outline our Think Beyond model and provide the overarching framework to help you navigate a PCM.

PART III

The
Think Beyond
model

7

Calm

The antidote to exhaustion isn't rest. It's wholeheartedness.
David Whyte

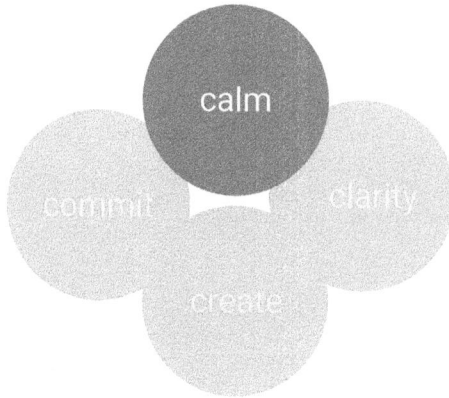

- **What:** An emergency break, a time focusing on self and feelings.
- **Why:** To calm down the amygdala response, tap into rational higher ordered thinking and bring positivity.
- **How:** By calming your body and mind, observing breathing, practising mindfulness and creating a space to reflect and rediscover joy.

Our Think Beyond model is based on four stages – calm, clarity, create and commit – and the chapters in this part provide strategies to use this model and successfully prepare for, cope with and move past your pivotal career moment (PCM). The overarching idea of Think Beyond is perspective. It's about self-awareness and the ability to create a new you. You are in a moment that passes – even though you might feel in the depths of that moment that it will never end. This model is designed to help you to think beyond. We will cover the first stage of the model in this chapter – calm.

As described in the earlier chapters, in a PCM, our research uncovered some typical stress responses during this time. If you are like most executive women, you tend to miss the first important step outlined in the Think Beyond model – to slow down before you can speed up.

What is the meaning of calm? According to Cambridge Dictionary calm is feeling 'peaceful, quiet, without worry; without hurried movement or noise'. Meriam Webster online dictionary describes calm as 'peaceful, tranquil, quiet and free from disturbance; calm is used when someone is not excited or upset, even when there is cause for it'. So what we're talking about here isn't an expectation that calm comes naturally. In the case of a PCM, you have every reason to not feel calm – especially when your confidence snowball creates anxiety and stress, as highlighted in our research. We need to be purposeful about being calm, and we discuss this further in this chapter.

First, we take you through an understanding of the neurobiology around calm and why calm matters for optimal thinking. We also outline the practical aspects of finding calm through self-compassion and how fitting the oxygen mask on ourselves will ultimately serve those around us.

Calm comes before clarity

The first stage in the Think Beyond model, calm, is like applying the emergency brake on the racing downhill pathway of your confidence snowball. Pulling the emergency brake requires consciousness, courage and determination. Depending on how fast your snowball is travelling downhill, it will be tough. But if you don't, this trajectory will end in a career avalanche. When you give yourself permission to rediscover yourself and your identity – inside and outside of work – your passions, strengths, skills, purpose and clarity will emerge.

Calm (and clarity, covered in the following chapter) are the foundations for the model. You cannot successfully visualise and build pathways unless you work through these stages. If you don't create a sense of calmness first, you risk making reactive decisions – jumping into a new role for the wrong reasons, for example, or hanging onto a role or organisation for reasons based on fear. This will speed up your spiralling lack of confidence snowball.

Vanessa, in coaching many senior executives, has noticed a pattern. They have been conditioned by the pace of executive demands, deadlines and self-imposed expectations. The biggest challenge Vanessa finds is getting executives to give themselves permission to slow down, look inward and rediscover themselves and what's important. When this process becomes a priority, there is an alignment with and trust in one's self, and newfound self-compassion. This elevates confidence and the ability to think beyond with optimism and positivity, as opposed to that snowballing lack of confidence, uncertainty and anxiety. It is a joy to be part of this transformation, and to see executive women move ahead in careers, with an authentic level of confidence.

Yasmin, who we introduced in part I, moved from a psychologically unsafe environment when she decided to leave her previous organisation. She took this as an opportunity and became disciplined enough to focus on calm. She took time to reconnect with herself and her family, and rebuilt priorities around what was important for her – including a complete stocktake around her internal and external wellbeing. From there, she could work on regaining clarity around what meant the most to her in her next career move. This resulted in a renewed sense of self-discovery, a renewal of her confidence and belief in her value and worth. Yasmin was coached using the four-stage Think Beyond model and framework we outline in this and the following chapters, and went on to achieve her dream job. She is now a CEO in an industry where she's kicking goals in areas she's passionate about: gender equality, industry representation (especially during and following COVID-19) and creating psychologically safe workplaces. This may not have been achieved if she didn't start with the first stage, calm.

✏ Reflection point

- What does calm mean to you?
- What enables you to feel 'calm'?
- Where are you?
- What are you doing?

Calm matters for optimal thinking

Shifting your body from the stressed state to the calm state allows you to make better decisions for your long-term future. Optimal thinking is the best thinking for you and your situation; it's thinking longer term, and not immediately responding to fear and perceived threats. It's not reacting but thinking strategically.

To understand a little more about optimal thinking, let's take a look at some of the science behind this. In chapter 2, we mentioned the area of our brain known as the limbic system. Commonly known as the emotional centre of the brain, this system is made up of a combination of structures including the amygdala, a pair of small almond-shaped structures. The amygdala is involved in the processing of emotions and memories associated with fear, and is a powerful reactionary centre in our brain designed to keep us safe and out of harm's way. When this region perceives a threat, it triggers the sympathetic nervous system to enter a state of high alert – fight or flight. However, your brain can't tell the difference between imagined and real threats. So when you are highly stressed, worried and/or ruminating about a situation at your work, your sympathetic nervous system still switches on. Stress neurochemicals such as adrenaline, norepinephrine and cortisol can be felt in action. The resulting symptoms from these hormones flooding the body were described by our interviewees in a variety of ways, including a racing heart, palpitations, feeling jittery, rushes of energy, sleep disturbances, perspiration, shallow and rapid breathing, increased blood pressure and heightened senses. We both have also felt such symptoms during a PCM. You might say you feel like you're on the edge. Our interviewee Anna, currently a CEO in the for-purpose sector with prior CEO experience in a top ASX-200 company and board director, provides a clear example here. She described times of incredible stress during her career, and even recalled a time where she suddenly lost taste and smell, which continued on to a disturbing metallic taste in her mouth. The amount of stress at that time appeared to trigger a neurological response impacting these sensory organs. This was an additional worry to Anna; however, she soldiered on as many executive women do.

Despite not being in a frame of mind to think optimally, many executive women told us they often attempted to keep ploughing through, continuing to work at a high pace in an attempt to make sense of what is happening during a PCM. When in this heightened state of stress, however, you are not able to tap into your prefrontal cortex – which is where your rational thinking and higher order executive brain functioning happens. This calm stage of the Think Beyond model is all about calming your emotional centre of the brain, and switching off stress overdrive to enable other centres of the brain – predominantly the prefrontal cortex – to operate effectively. Becoming calm is a different type of action, moving away from the usual 'jump in and take action' response that came through in our research. However, it does require prioritisation. Calm is also about activating the positive happiness neurochemicals – including oxytocin, dopamine, endorphins and serotonin – which have been proven to improve cognition, memory, motivation, attention and learning, and to regulate mood.

The research report 'The biochemistry of love: an oxytocin hypothesis' from Sue Carter and Stephen Porges goes so far as to say that oxytocin is like a hormonal 'insurance' against overwhelming stress. You need these 'happiness' neurochemicals during a PCM to prevent a lack of confidence and increasing stress snowball gathering mass and momentum as it heads downhill. Imagine these 'happiness' neurochemicals as providing a type of Teflon coating to help prevent the gathering of extra snow.

Calm is about awareness – awareness of your relationship with stress, awareness of your body and how you are feeling, and awareness of how you are balancing your eight wellbeing factors (that we discussed in chapter 5). This awareness gives you the information you need to prioritise the actions required for an improved state of being. Do not interpret the calm stage of our model as a 'nice-to-have'. It is essential in a PCM if you want to make a wise decision about the future and avoid a rash one.

As mentioned, a significant stress response during a PCM can reduce your ability to access the prefrontal cortex, which reduces your ability to activate rational thinking, critical reasoning and solid judgement. Stress and anxiety left unattended can also result in serious health implications – for example, increased blood pressure, increased risk of heart conditions and stroke. We always strongly recommend that you seek professional medical advice. Stress neuro-chemicals can interrupt your sleep. As discussed previously, sleep disturbance is one of the first signs of a PCM, and is proven to have a direct impact on your mood and ability to cope with stress.

If you do not start with calm and simply continue full steam ahead, you put your mental and physical wellbeing at risk. You also speed up a confidence snowball, make suboptimal decisions and, depending on the impact of the mood, put important relationships at risk.

Eliza, introduced in part I, tackled her PCM by shifting the focus back to herself and reframing her approach. She engaged her support crew, including her colleagues, and allowed herself to feel the love from others. This example demonstrates the need for con-nection and how connection boosts our feel good neurochemicals, which provides a buffer against stress. Coupled with a renewed focus on her health and wellbeing, Eliza was able to find calm, tap into her resilience with greater effectiveness and manage her stress during what was a significant PCM for her.

Vanessa also knows what a build-up of stress neurochemicals and hormones feels like. During the start of the COVID-19 pandemic she endured significant stress. She was pivoting to online coaching, working with displaced employees, managers and executives from global clients, as well as being isolated from her ageing parents. She experienced some alarming symptoms that resulted in her spending a night in hospital because the symptoms were initially misdiagnosed as a stroke. Vanessa thought the solution to her stress-related symptoms would be a gin and tonic. Alas, no! Her hospital trip is also a reminder that alcohol is not an effective relaxation remedy, though it is one that many turn to.

✏️ Reflection point

Visualise a time when you've been highly stressed – for example, when you were preparing for a board presentation, sitting an exam, finding out your role was being made redundant, or working through a restructure and/or change of reporting relationships.

Think carefully about the symptoms listed in this section. Did you notice any of these signs in your body? Take note of how you feel after thinking about that highly stressful situation. Do you feel any of those symptoms just thinking about the situation?

Your thought process and mental rehearsal can be interpreted as reality by your brain. Be aware that this may bring on unpleasant feelings.

This exercise is to illustrate a point, but it is also important to follow on with the next part of the exercise – provided in the 'Reflection point' box at the end of the next section.

Self-compassion brings calm

The practical aspects of finding calm come through self-compassion, which we discuss in chapter 5. Fitting the metaphorical oxygen mask on yourself first will ultimately help you and others around you. Self-compassion entails being warm and understanding towards yourself when you suffer, fail or feel inadequate, rather than ignoring your pain or flagellating yourself with self-criticism. When the reality of a PCM is denied or fought against, your suffering increases in the form of stress, frustration and self-criticism. This movement towards self-kindness, compassion and mindfulness is a continuation of what we outline in chapter 5, based on the work of Dr Kristin Neff.

As Harvard professor Amy Cuddy highlights, 'Our bodies change our minds, and our minds can change our behaviour, and our behaviour can change our outcomes'.

Our personal experience is that when you don't feel your best, you don't perform at your best. When feeling suboptimal, it's hard to think positively, focus objectively and cope with the stress that a PCM can inflict. Calm is about shifting the focus from external stresses and the harsh self-critic, bringing the focus back to self in a compassionate way, and prioritising a way for you to decompress, calm down, recompose, relax and step away from the pressure. Finding this calm state enables you to acknowledge what you are feeling and to sit with this versus rushing off and keeping busy. Self-compassion is about applying the best techniques to settle your hyper-stressed responses and find calm. We include one specific awareness technique in the 'Reflection point' box at the end of this section, but others are also available, including mindfulness, meditation, exercise, a healthy diet and lots of water, social connectivity, gratefulness journalling and good sleep, as well as listening to music, laughter and creativity. Ultimately, find some joy and reflect on this joy. None of these techniques is an instant fix. You have to commit yourself to making changes over time.

All these techniques are grounded in evidence-based research that continues as technology advances enable further studies. Vanessa completed neuroscientist Dr Sarah McKay's Foundations of Neuroscience program, where McKay provided learnings gathered from multiple research papers across these topics. Her content reinforced and validated this information for us. The adult brain can be changed (based on neuroplasticity and neurogenesis); the techniques discussed here promote positive neurochemicals that modulate and even protect parts of the brain from elevated stress. Mindfulness can literally rewire the brain to be calmer, present, healthier and happier.

Another evidence-based technique that is necessary when becoming calm (and also when transiting from calm to clarity, the topic of the next chapter) is understanding what you can and can't control. Dr Stephen Covey wrote *The 7 Habits of Highly Effective People* in 1989, but it is still one of the best reminders of the personal change journey. In particular, he talks about his circles of influence and concern. Covey's model of these two circles has been adapted now with a third circle – a circle of control. As you can see in figure 3, you need to question yourself around what you can control, what you may be able to influence, and what you may be concerned about but have no control or influence over. Areas you can control are those that are centred on how you choose to act, your behaviours and thoughts (or how you choose to deal with your thoughts), your attitude, and how you choose to show up to a situation. Areas you may have little or no control over include the changing economy, what others think, past decisions and the weather. If you spend all your time trying to fix, change, influence or stress about areas you have no control over, you will not find any resolution or peace.

Figure 3: Circles of control, influence and concern

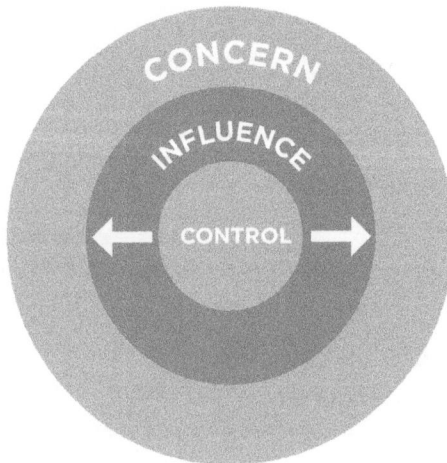

You need to be calm to make good decisions for your future, and self-compassion is the shortest route back to calm.

Coming back to our interviewee, Anna now uses physical exercise to manage her stress. She described how going for a walk or a swim, or even sitting in the sun for five minutes, changes her demeanour. She noticed how her emotional state and the emotional challenges she has had to deal with have a lot to do with her level of confidence, telling us, 'I find emotions affect your confidence. I draw a lot of strength from long-term relationships with my friends.' Anna describes the authenticity that is present in these relationships because they know each other so well, like having a good time with family. 'I've got a fantastic group of friends and that's where I go to redraw my strength.'

Anna's example, as with many of our executive interviewees, illustrates how important human connection with family and/or friends is, having a laugh and enjoying life – it's a good dose of the hormone oxytocin – which provides the calming effect.

✏ Reflection point

Here is the second part of the visualisation exercise introduced in the previous reflection point. Visualise your most relaxing holiday or favourite weekend away – a time when you applied self-compassion. The experience might include a massage, a walk on the beach or in nature, a lunch with friends, a yoga class, something you can laugh at on Netflix or an afternoon nap. What happens to those stress symptoms when you visualise these times? What do you notice about your demeanour? Write down those times and the things you love to do that bring a little joy. What can you do to reincorporate some of these moments back into your life? Even just imagining these joyful and calming activities changes your demeanour.

Finding your 'space'

We mentioned Stephen Covey earlier as the author of *The 7 Habits of Highly Effective People*. Covey also wrote the foreword for the book *Prisoners of Our Thoughts: Viktor Frankl's Principles for Discovering Meaning in Life and Work* by Dr Alex Pattakos. In his foreword, Covey uses these words to summarise the work of Frankl:

> *Between stimulus and response there is a space, and in that space is the power to choose. And it's in that choice that lies our growth and happiness.*

Dr Susan David is one of the world's leading management thinkers and an award-winning Harvard Medical School psychologist. She also refers to Viktor Frankl and the idea of 'the space'. In a discussion with Lisa Leong on the ABC podcast 'This Working Life', Dr David talks about her research and work on emotional agility. She highlights that when we are in the grip of emotions, our neurobiology hardwires us to react and respond to stimulus. Emotional agility, on the other hand, helps us to create 'the space' by creating a pause. It is about using this pause to decide how to act in this situation.

Asking yourself questions can help you unpack your real feelings and thoughts and create this space. What is going on? What am I feeling? What do I need to do in this situation that best serves me and aligns with how I want to show up? What values are really important to me and does my reaction and behaviour align with these values?

As an example of this, Ita Buttrose, 2013 Australian of the Year and one of Australia's most successful businesswomen, discussed her leadership style, especially during the tough roles she's undertaken. In a cover story for the *Australian Women's Weekly* in July 2022, she oozes her wisdom now in her 81st year, and describes 'the space' in action:

As you get older, you do understand people a lot better. I'm prepared to let things run and observe. I take time to act, to say what's on my mind. You don't always have (to) be in such a hurry.

When we are hooked by emotions, no space exists between stimulus and response – we feel something and we act immediately. By becoming emotionally agile, we create the pause and decide how to act in this situation.

Again, ask yourself calming questions to gain perspective. What is going on here? What am I feeling? What do I need to do in this situation? What are the values I hold to be really important?

✏ Reflection point

What do you do to create the 'pause' or the space that separates 'what's going on' from your reaction or response? When was a time when you were hooked by your emotions? Reflect back on the situation and your response. When this happens again, what will you do to create the space?

What are the values you hold that are important to you? Write them down. Are these the values that you use to make big decisions? Are these the values you benchmark yourself against?

Summing up

Your biology and brain prepare and prime you for threats to your safety – including your psychological safety. Your brain can interpret stressful situations as a threat and trigger a neurochemical chain reaction. This response doesn't set you up to think clearly, use your best judgement and make rational decisions during a PCM and confidence snowball.

Our Think Beyond model is in a specific order for this reason. Calm comes before clarity. The magic of calm comes when you can tap into your higher ordered, rational, strategic, less reactive, executive level thinking. Peel back your layers. Go beneath the superwoman cape and shield and regain connection with your values, identity, purpose and meaning. You are then ready for clarity – the topic of the next chapter.

8

Clarity

It takes as much energy to wish as it does to plan.
Eleanor Roosevelt

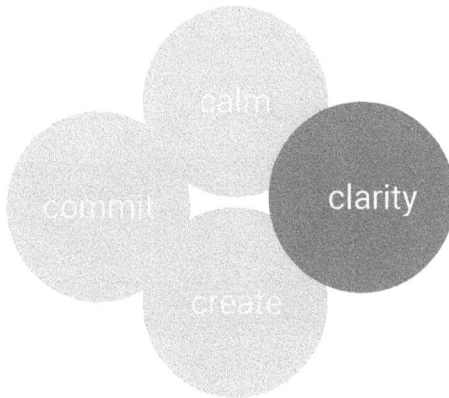

- **What:** An understanding of the real issue, fear, areas of control, strengths and gaps.
- **Why:** To find your pathway, reconnect with values, strengths and achievements, and gain a better sense of self.
- **How:** By reframing your narrative, purposefully identifying your values and strengths, and identifying what is important to you.

Clarity is defined by the Merriam-Webster Dictionary as the quality of being easily understood – the quality of being expressed, remembered and understood in an exact way, and of being easily seen or heard. In this chapter, take this definition and apply it to you – your understanding of self, and being able to hear and see yourself. Clarity, in this context, is shifting you from an ambiguous, uncertain and unclear state. It shines a light on the situation, the facts, the fears and where you fit in, with a focus on what you can and can't control. Until you cover these steps, you cannot authentically lift your sights wider to reconnect with your identity.

It takes courage to find clarity. In the following sections, we explore how to unblock to find the real you in this pivotal career moment (PCM), and how gaining clarity can build confidence through re-engaging connection with our values, strengths, skills, passion and purpose.

Finding clarity takes courage

Applying the calm stage of our Think Beyond model (refer to the previous chapter) enables you to stop and take a breath. You can then start exploring the second stage of the model – clarity. This stage is all about unpacking the blockers to find the real you among this PCM. Digging below the surface in this way requires courage. Without the clarity that comes from this process, executive women can feel uncertain and rudderless.

Through our research delving into the feelings of the executive women we spoke with, we discovered common blockers to finding the real you include self-doubt, feeling not worthy, fear of failure, perfectionism, worrying about what others think, fear of rejection or worrying about things outside of immediate control. These can be the same things that trigger your lack of confidence snowball in the first place. Exploring your blockers can only happen after you've peeled back your own layers to find the gold, which is clarity hidden beneath misinterpretation and negative beliefs. In this section, we challenge your fear by fact-checking and myth-busting these blockers.

If you don't understand the blockers to your clarity, moving to the next stages of create and commit (covered in the following two chapters) is difficult. You risk not truly understanding yourself, which is necessary to resolve a PCM, and being unable to bust the downward lack of confidence snowball.

Interviewee Anna, from the previous chapter, described her feelings about the imposter syndrome label within this context, and that in some cases the label isn't as negative as we might think. She describes the thinking behind the label as 'human beings understanding who we are and why we are doing what we are doing' or questioning why we are doing what we are doing. She describes the negative connotations around the imposter syndrome label as detracting from the benefit of unpacking or peeling back the layers. 'Imposter syndrome is a kind of self-reflective thing, and I have no issue with self-reflection.' Questioning who you are and how you got there – and where your strengths truly lie – takes courage. You are not questioning your worthiness, but questioning how well you know yourself. This provides clarity, and you need this before you can move forward.

✎ Reflection point

Blockers get in the way of you identifying your value. List those feelings and thoughts of self-doubt – including any thoughts on fear of failure, perfectionism and impostor syndrome – in your journal. Now, walk through your list one at a time with a reframe challenge.

Here are the steps in this process:

- How much of what you've listed is factually real? How much is built by old beliefs, worries or concerns?
- What is a different way to interpret this?
- Remove words such as 'should', 'always', 'never' and 'can't' from your response.
- What would your mentor or a close friend tell you about this interpretation?
- How is this interpretation blocking you from appreciating your authentic self?
- What can you learn from this new assessment that you can apply in further situations?
- What do you now understand about this fear?

Identifying strengths and values to find clarity

Once you have regained your calm, and identified and busted your blockers, you can now build clarity – a better understanding of yourself and the values, strengths, skills, passion and purpose that form your identity. Bringing this understanding into a conscious level is what drives trust in yourself. And trusting yourself is confidence building.

During a PCM, executives struggle to articulate their strengths. In Vanessa's coaching experience, executives have been busy getting stuff done and are not consciously aware of their toolkit of strengths they continually hone and draw upon. Vanessa also found executive women find this process of identifying strengths particularly tricky in comparison to executive men.

When in a PCM, it is easy to focus on your weaknesses versus your strengths. Reframing to focus on strengths is a way to regain deeper understanding of your value and potential, which in turn helps you steady the confidence snowball. Uncovering and focusing on strengths creates a more positive mindset, readying you for the next stage of the Think Beyond model – create, which we outline in the next chapter.

When asked the question 'What are your strengths?', many executive women fumble. This question is too broad and doesn't help you to uncover the detailed weave that makes up the fabric of your strengths. Many types of strength assessments are available, and some are more formal than others. The Gallup CliftonStrengths, Strength Deployment Inventory 2.0, Strengths Profile and VIA Character Strengths Survey are some examples. In *Average to A+: Realising strengths in yourself and others*, positive psychology expert Alex Linley highlights that 'when people talk about strengths, they are more positive, energetic, and engaged. Body language is open and receptive, and they are enthusiastic'. In other words, talking about your strengths creates a step forward in confidence-building clarity. Linley goes on to argue,

> When people are talking about weaknesses, they are more negative, hesitant, and disengaged. Their energy levels drop, and they appear more withdrawn. Their body language is closed and defensive, and their attentional focus is narrowed.

These reactions show strong similarities with our lack of confidence snowball and, as discussed, when in a PCM it is easy to focus on your weaknesses versus your strengths.

Based on Alex Linley's Individual Strengths Assessment process, the following questions can help put you in a mindset of strengths. Start your strengths discovery by asking yourself the following:

- What sort of everyday things do I enjoy doing?
- What makes for a really good day?
- What is the best day I can remember having?
- What would I describe as my most significant accomplishment?
- When am I at my best, what am I doing?
- What gives me the greatest sense of being authentic and who I really am?
- What do I think are the most energising things that I do?
- Where do I gain the most energy from?
- What sorts of activities am I doing when I feel most energised?
- What am I doing when I feel most invigorated?
- When was a time when I thought the real me was coming through?
- Do I have a vision for the future? And what is it about?
- What am I most looking forward to in the future?
- What will I be doing next week when I'm at my best?

In a *Psychology Today* article from 2021, Dr Ryan Niemiec (Chief Science & Education Officer at the VIA Institute on Character) makes an interesting correlation between values and character strengths. He states:

> *Many people ask about the connection between character strengths and values. I posit that 'values' live in our head – our thinking and feeling – and we hold our values (e.g., value for hard work or value for our family) dear to us. Values, however, do not say something about our behavior, whether or not we actually put those thoughts/feelings into action. That's where character comes in – the activation of our values.*

Your values will also emerge as you delve into the list of questions relating to your strengths just provided. Your values are the important principles and standards that underpin your judgement and decision-making. Values can shift over time as priorities and importance changes. You need to be conscious of your values, reconnecting with them, and holding them as your true north. Values are deeply personal. Values alignment and shared values draw us closer and create a sense of harmony and positivity, while values misalignment creates incongruence and discord. Left unattended, this misalignment can contribute to a confidence snowball. To activate your values, you need to be conscious and aware. Allowing time to reflect and reconnect is vital in this process.

✎ Reflection point

Work through the questions listed in this section and make notes and observations in your journal.

You may have completed other strengths assessments as part of your executive leadership development. Find them and review. If you can't find them or want to refresh, you can visit viacharacter.org to complete your VIA Character Strengths Survey. Which of these character strengths have enabled your success when in action?

Make a list of your values, and then challenge yourself to prioritise the top three. How do these play out for you in your life now? Can you see congruence or incongruence?

Gaining clarity to build confidence

As we detailed in chapter 1, confidence goes back to the Latin root *confedio* – having full trust. We interpret this as trusting yourself and your abilities, capability, judgement and gut. It's about trusting that you've been around the block a few times and that if you don't have all the answers, you know how to find out. It's also about accepting that vulnerability is okay – and trusting yourself anyway, and understanding your strengths and your appetite to learn and grow.

In our experience, gaining clarity enables you to celebrate and acknowledge your strengths, while assessing areas for growth and development. Providing you have allowed time for calm, this brings you one step closer to having a growth mindset. As well-known psychologist and author Carol Dweck describes, having a growth mindset enables you to identify gaps in performance and view these as opportunities in a positive and non-threatening way – rather than with the self-doubt and fear that fuel a lack of confidence snowball.

When coaching, Vanessa encourages executives to tell stories of their proud career moments, and of the achievements, no matter how big or small, that are meaningful to them. The next step is a deeper look into what underpinned those moments and achievements, including the key strengths and personal qualities that enabled these outcomes. Executives always discover more about themselves through telling these stories. These insights start to unleash a greater holistic awareness, clarity and confidence around what makes them successful.

If you don't know who you really are, determining the right pathway forward in your career will be hit or miss. In our experience, when executives choose pathways without clarity, they risk incongruence between the new organisation or role and their personal values and goals. This can leave executives feeling anywhere between uncomfortable to deeply unsatisfied. This is a perfect situation for a confidence snowball, and potential career avalanche.

Our interviewee Catherine provides a good example here. Catherine's career included senior executive roles within a large and complex government organisation, leading a range of functions – from customer strategy, corporate services and company secretary, to people and culture. When she was hit by a PCM, her confidence was rocked. Well-intentioned friends and ex-colleagues were quick to suggest new roles and opportunities, and she felt pressure to immediately take on another big executive role. She felt conflicted, still feeling battered and bruised by her career avalanche. Coaching support enabled Catherine to give herself permission to elevate 'calm' as a priority, and she took some time to understand herself after her PCM. She put in place a complete stocktake around her wellbeing, and appreciated the importance and necessity of finding calm before racing into an exhaustive job search process.

Slowing down, and fully extracting herself emotionally from her previous organisation took time. Further support carefully peeled back the layers to help Catherine understand what was important to her, and reconnect with her confidence anchor points – her values, strengths, skills, passion and purpose. She then moved to the next stage of our Think Beyond model, to work out what was next and commit to her goal. We cover this stage in the next chapter, but – spoiler alert – Catherine did secure a CEO role in a not-for-profit organisation, in an area she is passionate about. This is an example of the importance of time and focusing on calm then clarity. Work out what's important to you and what brings you purpose and meaning before forging ahead, post-PCM.

✐ **Reflection point**

This next piece can be tricky and requires thinking time. (It isn't a timed quiz!) Make notes, drawings, mind maps in your journal as you tackle these questions:

- How do you describe your identity?
- How would you describe yourself outside of work?
- Where do you find purpose and meaning?

These can be tricky questions for time-poor executives, but find the time and space to answer them calmly and with clarity.

Summing up

Clarity requires you to be courageous. Clarity gives you better understanding as it reconnects you with your values, strengths and achievements, and gives you a better sense of yourself. Clarity reconnects you with your confidence anchor points.

Don't shy away from clarity. Identify the real issues and blockers. Challenge fear and assumptions. Give up trying to control the uncontrollable and understand and embrace your strengths, skills and gaps. Remind yourself of your values and how you can activate these. Embrace Carol Dweck's lessons around a growth mindset. A PCM is an opportunity to learn and grow. Understand the importance of finding the authentic you and what makes you truly shine. Do this before making decisions about what's next.

Now we have positioned you with an ability to tap into your superpowers (which includes knowing your strengths, skills, values, purpose and meaning) you are ready to do what most executives do well – work out creative solutions. The next chapter continues through our Think Beyond model, enabling you to think beyond your PCM and determine future opportunities with confidence and commitment for success.

9

Create

What you get by reaching your goal is not as important as
what you become by reaching your goals.
Zig Ziglar

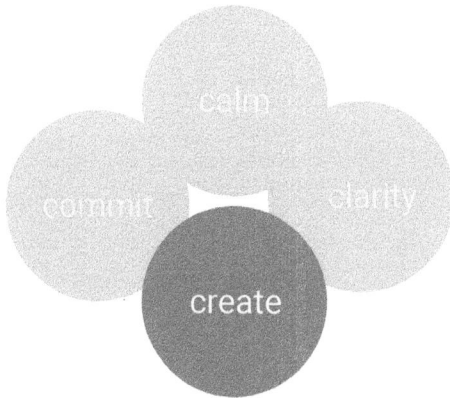

- **What:** An opportunity to think beyond, to see possibilities and create the future.
- **Why:** To build positivity around options, believe in a future pathway and create tangible steps to move forward.
- **How:** By creating an environment for visualisation and brainstorming, and setting smart goals.

Just a quick recap: when you are calm, it creates space for clarity. Now you're going to use that clarity to create a new plan for your future and something that you can act on. Your success in moving through a PCM relies on your ability to execute your new plan. Execution will depend on your focus and commitment to the changes needed to move ahead.

As you now know, experiencing a PCM rocks your confidence. We've highlighted the need to identify the things in and out of your control to avoid the lack of confidence snowball effect. We want you to recognise and understand that you are in control of your future. It's up to you to create and commit to that new future and continue your successful career.

Executives have told us that their PCM moments pushed them to dig deep and think about what they really wanted to do next. They shared with us how at times it was a very stressful situation. But once they understood that it was a process and they could move past it, it became a time when they reflected, learned a lot about themselves and became better executives.

The next stage in the Think Beyond model is to create your new path. Creating is an opportunity to think beyond, to see possibilities and create the future. This stage is necessary to build positivity around options, believe in a future pathway and create tangible steps to move forward. Merriam-Webster Dictionary defines create as 'to make or bring into existence something new; to produce or bring about by a course of action or behaviour'.

This stage is about creating new goals to guide your focus and help you sustain momentum to affect positive change. Goals motivate you to take action across all areas, including your wellbeing underpinning your personal and professional success. However, success is dependent on your efforts in completing the first two stages – to get calm and seek clarity first. The create and commit stages help you move past your PCM and avoid any confidence snowballs regaining momentum. As we've discussed, if you can't move past the PCM, you risk your lack of confidence and stress and anxiety snowballing to a career avalanche. Your health and wellbeing may be at risk. You may also face burnout, or may not return to the workforce at all, or return to an unsatisfying job. At a personal level, this can impact your brand, your financial position, your lifestyle and, most importantly, your wellbeing. At a macro level, it contributes to fewer women at executive level in the workforce. Progress towards gender equality in the C-suite or in the boardroom slows down (more on this in chapter 11).

We introduced you to Sally, an entrepreneur, business owner and author with 30 years' experience across financial services and the media, in chapter 2, and described how she found herself in a PCM. It was devastating for her. However, the experience forced her to think about how to revaluate her career and goals. At the time, she described it as a stressful situation, but giving herself the opportunity to be calm, and to take time out, created clarity. In her create stage, she creatively looked at her new future, came up with options, and set new goals and a pathway forward. She pivoted her business model from creating marketing content on demand to a whole new service and product offering – education and storytelling. Today she's even more successful. She has a sustainable business model, and enjoys a better lifestyle.

All of the executives we interviewed attributed the success of moving past their PCM to having new goals and a focus and commitment to stick to and deliver their plan. As a result, they are all in more successful positions – either in more senior roles, desired industry sectors or in their own business, elevating their credibility, expertise and personal brand.

In this chapter, we talk about the important steps to creating your new future. You need to take a holistic approach to setting career goals and they need to be revisited and confirmed for each life cycle and life stage.

Create your future – think beyond.

Step 1: Create a vision of your future

Create means to bring something into existence, and it's how you make sense of life events and impacts. This creative process is about relationships and your relationship with yourself. A PCM is a life event that happens to you. It's a process, with some aspects in and out of your control. However, in your complete control is how you respond to your PCM, and how you create this new future.

The first important create step is to visualise your future. A good reference point is to think about where you'd like to be in five years' time. What vision do you see? If you were creating a future on a blank canvas, what would it feature? Stretch yourself to think beyond a fixed mindset and delve into possibilities. Check your wellbeing balance wheel from chapter 5 to ensure you are visualising the holistic you. Stretching your mind to five years out will also help you brainstorm possibilities. This vision will act as your anchor point when you come to setting goals and action plans to get to that desired state.

You might be stuck in the moment and not thinking beyond the current environment, or what you need to do, grow and learn over the next five years.

When Marianne was in this moment, a very senior executive who she respected gave her some great advice. They said, 'Marianne, before you even think about what type of role you want, aligning to your vision and aligning to your values is a simple two by two matrix. Use this matrix to think about two important elements. The first is how much money do you need? What's your financial situation? The second is how much prestige do you want, or how do you appease your ego?'

Let's work through this matrix here. From a financial perspective, if you need the same amount of money (or more) than your current position provides, that will dictate what type of role or position you need in the future. If you like the prestige that your executive role brings, your next role needs to be higher or equal in prestige to your current role. As you move down the matrix – as your financial position changes, or your need for the prestige of that big C-suite role changes – you can start exploring other possibilities and other industries. Perhaps you can even consider roles in not-for-profit or for-purpose organisations, and see how you can spend some time doing important and meaningful work.

This two by two matrix helped Marianne think about how she could align with what she wanted to do, based on these needs. From a financial perspective, she needed to contribute to her household budget. From an individual perspective, she evaluated how she was perceived in the role that she had and the importance of that prestige. The financial side was being managed – Marianne has worked since she was 14 years and nine months, and when she learnt about compound interest from her year 10 maths teacher (bless you, Mr Hollowell) she instantly was a disciplined saver. The ego a role brings was also not her main driver. She wanted to do purposeful work so that she could continue contributing to businesses, continue her advocacy work, help people reach their potential and also learn and grow in herself. This matrix helped Marianne take what was important to her (as assessed by her during the clarity stage of our model), and prompted her to explore options. This resulted in her creating her portfolio career.

Once you've thought about where you lie on the financial/prestige matrix, the next step is to think about your values and your passions.

The closer you are to creating a future that aligns with your values and passions, the more motivated and excited you will be to move to the next career stage. Sometimes a PCM can be caused (at least in part) because of a misalignment between your role or company you work for and your values and passions. Using the perspective gained from the Think Beyond model, you can better align with what you want. Creating the right environment, space and time is essential for you to re-envisage your future. Use this to identify the transferability of key strengths and skills that you rediscovered in the previous chapter. Think about what you enjoy doing and how those strengths and skills can be used or transferred to other roles or to other industries. You've acquired so much in your career. Some skills will be transferable while other skills will need to be developed, but sitting and thinking about them will help you determine that next step.

Brainstorm options you may not have previously entertained. This broadens your thinking and creates a new, exciting passion and motivation to identify possibilities of your future. You're not limited just to where you have been today.

✏️ Reflection point

You may like to start with a complete blank canvas and create your own picture of the future. If that is a little daunting, you can use the questions in figure 4 to envisage your future five years from now.

Figure 4: Holistic Wellbeing model

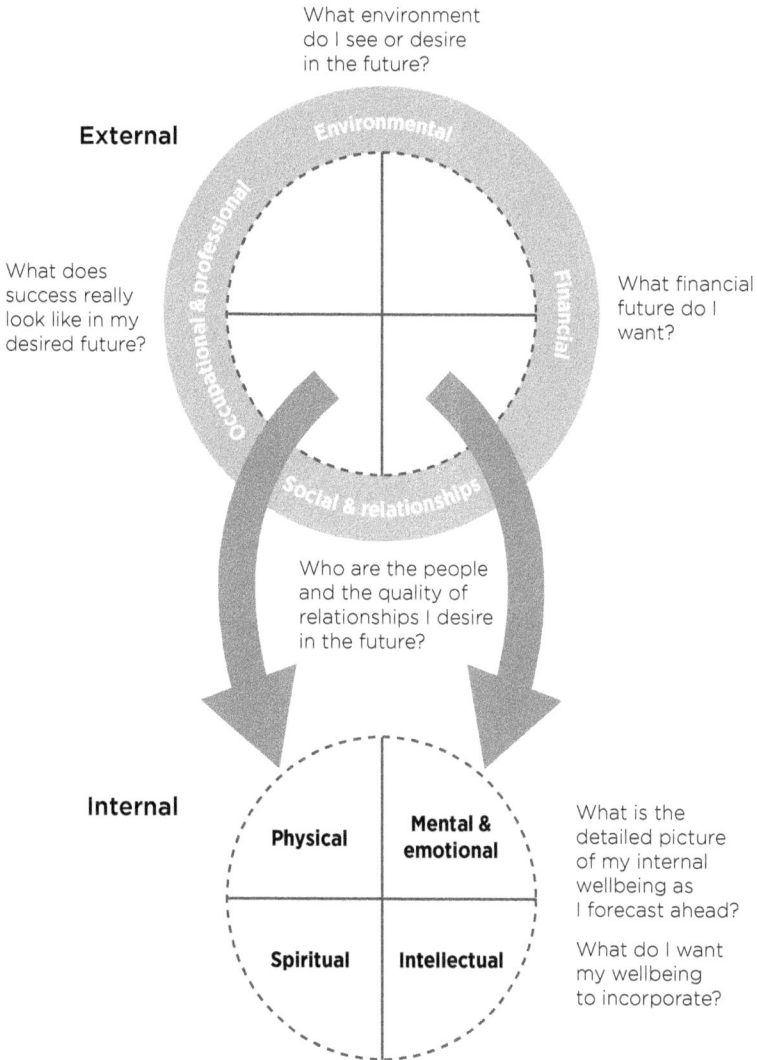

What environment
do I see or desire
in the future?

External

Environmental

Occupational & professional

Financial

Social & relationships

What does
success really
look like in my
desired future?

What financial
future do I
want?

Who are the people
and the quality of
relationships I desire
in the future?

Internal

Physical	**Mental & emotional**
Spiritual	**Intellectual**

What is the
detailed picture
of my internal
wellbeing as
I forecast ahead?

What do I want
my wellbeing
to incorporate?

Step 2: Create new goals

The Oxford Dictionary defines a goal as the object of a person's ambition or effort. It's a destination, an aim. This implies that you need physical or mental energy over this time to attain this goal. Goal setting is an important process in the create step.

Goal theory has been around for centuries – it's nothing new. Some of the first empirical studies were published in the 1930s by British philosopher Cecil Alec Mace. Fast-forward to today and Amazon has over 9000 results when we searched for 'goal setting books'. One of the most cited studies on goal performance and task performance was outlined in 'Goal setting and task performance: 1969–1980', published in 1981 in *Psychological Bulletin*. The authors of this article reported:

> *The effects of goal setting on performance show that in 90% of the studies, specific and challenging goals led to higher performance than easy goals, 'do your best' goals, or no goals. Goals affect performance by directing attention, mobilizing effort, increasing persistence, and motivating strategy development. Goal setting is most likely to improve task performance when the goals are specific and sufficiently challenging.*

The importance of having a goal is it gives you a clear focus point on what you want to achieve. The drive you then have to achieve your goals is a source of motivation that provides you fuel and will power you through challenging times. This means you need to set goals with enough stretch to keep you attentive and engaged. Without goals, it's easy to get distracted by the things that you cannot control or are less important to you. This then encourages negative self-talk, and that lack of confidence snowball can start building up again. Goals also give you focus to ensure you put your energy into the right things and move past your PCM.

Goals make you accountable. They create a positive pressure to ensure you stay on track and avoid the negative confidence snowball. Goals also help you achieve your full potential. Once you're clear about your goals, you can build your pathway to your future. Creating an emotional connection to your goal creates energy. This could include imagining how you will feel when you reach that point – including the excitement, the accomplishment or the satisfaction. This is an important step when creating goals that will inspire you to continue through the predictable challenges.

Breaking down your goals into actionable steps will help you move more quickly to your new future. Goals will help you break away from being caught in the narrow and short-term focus caused by the lack of confidence snowball. When you believe you have a pathway forward, you can commit to acting. If you don't create new goals, you will not reach your full potential. This is because you lack focus, have no priorities, easily get distracted and are busy doing the things that will not help you move past this PCM. The end result is that you'll miss opportunities, you won't progress and you'll move from a lack of confidence snowball to a career avalanche.

Marianne has experienced firsthand the importance of goal setting to help focus and hold you accountable to the future you. In 2019, after a really big year at work, she took a break with her family. While she was away from the hustle and bustle of work, she had the opportunity to create her personal calm. She also reflected on what she wanted to do in the next stage of her career. This was her own personal PCM. She knew the next steps over 2020 would be to find clarity through re-evaluating her strengths and skills and reconnecting with her values and passion.

At the start of 2020, in a year where the world became so uncertain with COVID-19 impacts, it would've been easier for Marianne to stay in her executive role. However, she decided where she wanted to transition her career – from a C-suite executive role to a portfolio career – and decided to start the move. She started to imagine where she could be and what joy that would bring her. She then wrote down her vision and her re-imagined future. She created new options and completed the matrix to set her new goals.

One of the first things Marianne did was reconnect with her support crew. She took this opportunity to learn from others who had followed a similar path. This gave her the opportunity to create her new goals, but putting the required steps into action was also important. Each step was built using the SMART framework, which, once you are calm and you have the clarity you need, is a useful approach. It makes sure that your goals are specific (S), measurable (M), attainable (A), relevant (R) and time bound (T). This process ensured that Marianne could navigate her PCM and focus on thinking about the key actions to create this new path.

We referred to the neuroscience that supports the Think Beyond model in chapter 7, and in particular the scientific reasons you need to find calm first, and then allow clarity to come. This evidence also supports the create stage. Dr Sarah McKay (refer to chapter 7) talks about how our brains do not like uncertainty. Having goals creates rigour in our focus. However, if your goal is too large or too distant, you run the risk of uncertainty and self-doubt. Acknowledging progress and achievement by ticking off the sub-goals and milestones triggers the rewarding neurotransmitter dopamine. When your brain registers this satisfaction, it produces a reward response that motivates you to keep going.

✏ Reflection point

Get started by setting your goals. First, let's start with your big picture or higher goal. This is what you're working towards over the next five years. For example, your goal may be to move to a more senior role. The next step is to list in your journal three or four sub-goals to help you achieve that new goal. For example, to move to a more senior role, some smaller steps might be to expand your network, or to enhance your existing skills – such as building leadership skills.

Review the goals you have written down. Create an emotional connection to each goal. What will it feel like when you have reached the goal? What will you be doing? How will you acknowledge your goal achievement?

Now you are ready to move into building your action plan.

Step 3: Create your strategy

As defined in the Oxford Dictionary, strategy is 'a plan of action designed to achieve a long-term or overall aim'. Creating your action plans will enable you to achieve your SMART goals.

This step assesses your goals against the current reality. Where are you right now? What is the gap and what are the specific actions to bridge that gap? As the old saying goes, 'The devil is in the detail'. While still in the create stage of our Think Beyond model, allow yourself the space to go deeper and explore the options, ideas, possibilities and mindset that will form part of your strategy to achieve your SMART goals.

In preparing a strategy to achieve her goal of moving to a portfolio career, Marianne engaged her support crew as a source of information, learning and support. Understanding what you know and what you don't know is essential. If your goals have enough challenge and stretch, then your strategy will involve leaning into actions that may feel uncomfortable. That is good! This discomfort can be one of your personal indicators of growth and learning. You are moving outside your comfort zone. The challenge is to acknowledge yourself positively for this progress versus gravitating back to what came naturally. Actions around acknowledgement can form part of your strategy. (We discuss self-reflection and feedback in the next chapter.)

Anticipating where your strategy may come unstuck will help you prepare for potential derailers. This includes identifying the triggers, emotions, environment and self-talk that may get in the way. For example, you may have a tendency to say 'yes' to other projects because they sound appealing. The result of this decreases your time and energy to focus on your goals. Armed with this insight, prepare for this scenario in advance. Ask yourself, 'What will I do to keep myself on track when something interesting pops up?' Identify this as part of your strategy.

Marshall Goldsmith is a psychologist, executive coach and author. His book *Triggers: Sparking positive change and making it last* suggests identifying both the negative and positive triggers that affect our behaviours is a successful strategy to keeping you on track to achieve your goals. As well as the potential derailers, identify the strategies that will keep you focused and your mindset positive. This may include creating the right environment, having prompts and reminders pop up or be visible, scheduling catch-ups with your support crew or joining groups with the same focus. As an example of this, actively participating in the cohort study group helped Vanessa keep focused and on top of the assignments required to complete the Company Directors Course through the Australian Institute of Company Directors (AICD). Another strategy is to engage an executive coach.

✍ Reflection point

Create a gap analysis by looking at your planned goals and your current reality. List the actions that will bridge the gap.

Think about the actions that you need to meet those goals, and write those in your journal. An example for expanding your network may be reviewing your existing network for any potential introductions or new connections. Can you join any associations or attend any functions to start creating these new networks? Remember to use the SMART framework when reviewing your goals. If they aren't realistic or achievable, you need sub-goals supported by a detailed strategy.

Prioritise the list and translate this into your master strategy document. Write this in your journal or keep it somewhere as a constant visual reminder – for example, an A3 sheet on your home office wall or even as your screen saver!

Summing up

Through this chapter (and the preceding two chapters), we've outlined how following the Think Beyond model is your guide to moving past your PCM. Creating your vision, goals and strategy is a vital step in this model, and will help ensure that you move past this PCM and continue with your successful career.

Make sure that you don't limit yourself with your goals. Stretch yourself. The further that you stretch yourself, the more you will learn and the more you will strive for what you want to achieve. This will help you navigate through your PCM, seeing it as a process as you move to your future state. The final stage in this process is to commit to your plan, which we cover in the next chapter.

10

Commit

The only limit to the height of your achievements is the reach
of your dreams and your willingness to work for them.
Michelle Obama

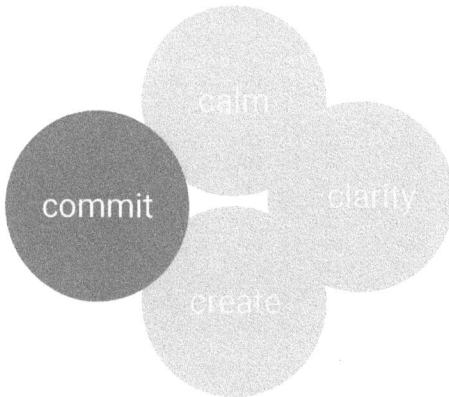

- **What:** An application of new thinking, mindset and commitment strategies.
- **Why:** To gain momentum and embed new habits, monitor and evaluate success, and prevent derailment.
- **How:** By taking action, creating a feedback and self-regulation process, and engaging support.

In this chapter, we want you to acknowledge the baggage that you'll need to leave behind to commit to focusing on the actions to achieve your new goals. Your goals need to be aligned to a self-regulatory cycle of action and performance assessment (and perhaps modification). You need to confirm your understanding and belief in who you are. According to the Merriam-Webster Dictionary, to commit means 'to carry into action deliberately; to pledge or assign to some particular course or use'. We also believe commit is to act – to gain momentum, build resilience and keep that confidence crisis at bay.

Commit to self-regulation

Now that you've created your new goals and plan, the most important step is to commit. Commit means action. A commitment only in your mind is just your imagination – it's only a dream. A goal is something that you commit to act on. If you don't act on that goal, nothing will happen. Without commitment, you will not succeed.

In this step, you need to adopt your new mindset and put into place what you know and have learned about yourself to reach the future that you want to move towards. It is important to understand that this step is hard and you may feel uncomfortable, or even anxious. When you feel this way, remember the first stage of the Think Beyond model (chapter 7) and check in on your level of calm.

A good way to keep track is to create a space and time for self-regulation. Self-regulation sits at the heart of your ability to make the change, move past the PCM and maximise your full potential. Self-regulation is a process by which you set your goal, develop the best plan of action, start that action and then monitor your performance. You evaluate your continuing performance by comparing it to your strategy. Based on this evaluation, you can modify or change your actions to further enhance your performance or better reach your goals. Figure 5 is based on the work of Professor Anthony Grant, recognised as a key pioneer of coaching psychology and evidence-based approaches to coaching.

Figure 5: Commit to a goal through taking action and then monitoring your performance

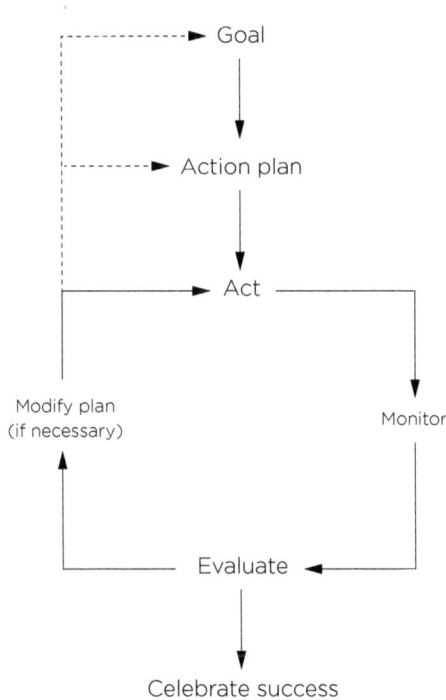

```
          ┌----------▶ Goal
          ┊              │
          ┊              ▼
          ┊----------▶ Action plan
          ┊              │
          ┊              ▼
          ┌──────────▶ Act ──────────┐
          │                          │
          │                          ▼
    Modify plan                   Monitor
    (if necessary)
          ▲                          │
          │                          │
          └────────── Evaluate ◀─────┘
                         │
                         ▼
                  Celebrate success
```

An important step in this process is the feedback loop. Without feedback on how you are tracking with your new actions and goals, you may not be able to keep modifying and acting, and so make that positive, purposeful change that you want and need to move past your PCM. This can be achieved by self-reflection to develop self-awareness and insight. Also important to note is the need to celebrate success along the way! If you have a tendency towards perfectionism and are a hard task master to yourself, it is even more important to reflect positively and build resilience to continue on your journey.

Commit to seeking feedback

A research study out of Japan (outlined in the article 'How self-determined choice facilitates performance: A key role of the ventromedial prefrontal cortex') looked at participants' brain activity while performing either a self-determined task or a task assigned without choice. The results showed that the negative reward value (identified on the fMRI brain scans) associated with negative feedback vanished when the participant was in a self-determined choice condition. Hence, to maintain progress towards your goals, it is critical to offset the negative emotional value of failure by treating the feedback informationally. This involves embracing a growth mindset, and focusing on the positive experience of using feedback as information to enhance future performance, in a self-determined way.

You can gain feedback in a self-determined and proactive way using several methods, including engaging your support crew and getting the help of an executive coach. This important feedback will help you align the changes of behaviour that you need to move you past the PCM and set you on a successful path for the future. When you get this self-insight and feedback, you have to continually assess and evaluate your action plans and time frames. Change what isn't working and make sure that you do more of what is working for you. Focus on your strengths and harness them positively to help you accelerate your development.

Commit to a new mindset

As covered in the previous chapter, breaking down your goals into smaller sub-goals will help you achieve that higher goal. It also helps you build that positive self-efficacy and will move you closer towards your higher goal. Once you start achieving smaller steps, you'll see the progress and the development, and other people will start to pick up on these changes as well. That builds your self-efficacy, making you feel positive, and motivating you to improve and make more of those changes. Remember to be kind to yourself. Self-compassion is important. Listen to your own narrative when assessing progress.

Watch out for 'I should have done this', or 'I've failed to achieve that'. You can flick back to chapter 1 for some examples of how to reframe any negative self-talk still creeping in.

Refocus on what commitment means to you, and reframe your language. Awareness, learning, growth and modification enable you to keep on track. This journey is self-determined, not assigned without choice. You are in the driving seat. These changes that you are making are big changes and you need commitment and focus. Any transformation or transition takes time, and is difficult to do alone.

Your success in moving past your PCM will depend on your commitment to your plan and goals by implementing monitoring systems to evaluate your success. You're going to shift from a fixed mindset to a growth and learning journey. Without commitment, you are unlikely to realise your goals and more likely to not move past that PCM. If you don't create and commit to your future, you'll get stuck doing the same thing and you won't move ahead. You'll continue the negative spiral and stay in a job or a position that you are not feeling passionate about. You'll lose motivation, and that can creep into your personal life as well.

In our experience, one of the reasons people fail to move past their PCM is because they don't set the right goals, or they have too many goals that don't push them to build that positive self-efficacy. They don't really commit to any of these goals or have the clear action to make things happen. They don't create that feedback loop to re-evaluate and make changes and adjustments along the way. This process is agile. You are learning about yourself and learning new things. You're tapping into the right people in your support crew, and asking them to give you valuable feedback. Have an agile mindset to make the changes that you need as you go along the way. You don't want to invest a lot of time, get to the end and then realise that it wasn't the outcome that you needed.

If you start to doubt yourself, you also end up in a 'paralysis by analysis' state – questioning every moment and thinking about every item. Watch out for procrastination, which may be linked to fear, anxiety or self-doubt creeping back in. If you feel the lack of confidence snowball starting to build, you need to get back into that calm state where you'll get the clarity you need (the first two stages of the Think Beyond model). You can't do the create and commit stages until you feel calm and have that clarity. This may take you longer than you expect. Give yourself the time that you need.

Commit to action, not reaction

Our survey results told us that 65 per cent of respondents in a confidence crisis jump to action without proper planning. When you jump into action, you can be doing the wrong actions. You'll have lots of activity and you'll be busy, but you'll likely not be focused on the right things. The commit stage is about taking action. But jumping in too early is not 'action'; it is a 'reaction'. Implementing the actions outlined in your strategy is your key to achieving your desired goal.

Anna, who we introduced in chapter 7, didn't stop to think about her next purposeful move when in a PCM, and instead moved straight into a new job. Three months into that role, she realised she'd made a mistake and the role wasn't aligned to her vision or her purpose. Because of the commitment she'd made to staying in that role and because she didn't want to let people down, Anna stayed in the role for another 12 months, which took a toll on her wellbeing. This trigger forced her to stop because she was feeling stressed and anxious – and even (as discussed in chapter 7) lost her sense of taste because of the stress.

When she finally left the role she'd jumped into, she created calm and took some time out to focus on her wellbeing. During that period, she got her health back on track and that gave her time and space to get the clarity that she needed about the next step that she wanted to do. Once that was clear, she set herself goals and actions. Six months later, Anna landed her dream job – CEO of a not-for-profit. She's thriving in that role and loving the opportunity. This example aligns with our experience that executives who create calm get the clarity they need to create and commit to a brighter future.

The Think Beyond model guides you through these four stages. Calm creates space for the clarity that you need. Once you have clarity, you're in a position to create the vision of your new future. When you're creating new goals, the SMART framework can help you. After you create, the final step is to commit and take action. This action will help move you to your future state.

An important component of the Think Beyond model is the self-regulation element. This is not always a linear process. You may get to the create stage and find yourself feeling stressed and anxious. Take yourself back to the calm stage, reassess, think about what's important, align to those visions and values that you have, and then progress through the model again.

✎ Reflection point

Take your new goals and build in the important feedback step. Think about where you can get feedback along the way at different points. Remember – you can seek feedback from your support crew or your executive coach, as well as building time into your day for self-reflection.

Try the daily reflection questions outlined by Marshall Goldsmith in his book *Triggers: Sparking positive change and making it last*. The questions included in table 3 are based on his insightful work. You can use these as your monthly commitment device, adding other questions as required. Also remember the words of Robert Collier: 'Success is the sum of small efforts repeated day in and day out'.

Now think about your lack of confidence snowball triggers. If they pop up, how will you deal with them? Make any adjustments that you need to and write these down. You now have your plan for your future.

Table 3: Daily reflection questions

List your questions to monitor your action and inaction. Every evening for one month write down a score between 0 and 10. When you notice a pattern of inaction forming, review your strategy and understand your blockers. The earlier you catch this, the quicker you can intervene and get back on track.

Did I do my best to: (the behaviour you wawnt to change/maintain)	1	2	3	4	5	6	7	8	9	10	11	12	13	14	15	16	17	18	19	20	21	22	23	24	25	26	27	28	29	30	31
work on an action from my desired future strategy plan?																															
implement my planned wellbeing actions?																															
engage with someone important to me for this journey?																															
adapt a positive and growth mindset?																															
learn something that supports my progress?																															
avoid distraction during my focus work blocks?																															

Summing up

Well done. You've created your new future and are ready and motivated for success and exciting times ahead. The focus of this book has been about how you can make the changes you need to move through your PCM in order to continue your own successful path. Through the Think Beyond model, you've created calm, you've got clarity, you've created goals that support your new future and now you are ready to commit – to consciously take action, motivated and ready for the exciting opportunities ahead. It's important to make these changes so that you'll feel more confident and continue to progress with your successful career.

Before we finish up, we want to give you one last chapter to provide a reality check of the bigger picture. This book has focused on you, but remember: you are part of a bigger system. What we want to focus on in the next chapter is the macro and social factors that are at play in the corporate system and are working against the progression of women. Without the awareness of these factors, we see too many women not achieving their goals. Collectively we can make changes, or we'll continue to have fewer women in senior roles. We all can play a critical role in turning these dire statistics around, and creating meaningful change for the next generation.

11

The social and community impacts of the current corporate system

Empowering women isn't just the right thing to do –
it's the smart thing to do.
President Barrack Obama

You now better understand and recognise the impact of pivotal career moments (PCMs) on your confidence and career, and have the strategies and knowledge to navigate through them. However, we couldn't end our book without giving you a more macro view to help you understand your confidence crisis in the context of some of the systematic issues working against you and other women.

The first thing to know is that the impacts of a confidence crisis snowball may extend beyond you as an individual, so don't be hard on yourself. The statistics we discuss in this chapter tell us that women are less represented in executive and leadership roles and on boards, in Australia and globally. This points to a systemic issue and a societal issue – and, importantly, we can all have an impact in turning the system around. Doing so is not only important for women, but also an important economic issue.

Deloitte's 2022 report *Breaking the Norm* found that more flexible ideas around gender norms could lead to an additional $128 billion each year for Australia's economy, and 461,000 additional full-time employees. We are not suggesting that you carry the banner for every woman in the workplace. The only person that you can control is yourself. But this is an opportunity for you to make a contribution to a wider issue, should you choose to take a broader interest and become a role model for the future generation of inspiring women – because you can't be what you can't see.

The current state of play

As mentioned back in chapter 1, when our survey respondents were asked to nominate a leader who exuded confidence, only one of the top four nominated was a woman, despite the predominantly female sample. Around a third of women chose a male leader, yet only a single man chose a female leader. This was despite these men knowing that the research we were undertaking was about executive women and confidence. They still chose male leaders as confident role models. What does this tell us about leadership perceptions and unconscious bias?

This also played out in one of our interviews with Amelia, former CEO and now non-executive director and chair for a number of ASX-listed organisations, who we introduced in chapter 1. She spoke of 'you can't be what you can't see'. If people don't see women in senior roles, they'll continue to form a male bias for these roles. Amelia is a passionate role model and encourages women to step up, and build resiliency and support systems to stay in these roles.

Now, we're going to share with you some of the depressing facts and figures.

Workplace Gender Equality Agency (WGEA) 2022 statistics show that women make up less than half of the employed persons in Australia (47.9 per cent), with 21.6 per cent of women working part-time. This means Australian women's earning capacity is automatically reduced. Further, women still earn significantly less than men across the Australian workforce. The current gender national pay gap difference between women's and men's average full-time base salary in Australia is 14.1 per cent. The gap widens to 22.8 per cent for total remuneration when superannuation, bonuses and other additional payments are factored in.

These two factors have a significant impact on the retirement savings of women. Women are retiring with approximately 65 per cent of the superannuation balance of men, as found by KPMG in their 2021 report *Addressing the Gender Superannuation Gap*.

Chief Executive Women (CEW) explored these gaps and inequalities even further in their 2022 *CEW Senior Executive Census*. Their key finding was that the progress on women reaching the most senior leadership roles in corporate Australia is going backwards. At the current rate of progress, it will take 100 years for women to make up at least 40 per cent of all CEO positions on the ASX-200.

Some other findings from the *CEW Senior Executive Census* include:

- More ASX-300 companies have no women in their executive leadership teams than the previous year (46 in 2022, compared to 44 in 2021).
- Fewer ASX-300 companies have gender balanced executive leadership teams (50, down from 58 in 2021).
- Of 28 CEO appointments at ASX-300 companies in the past year, only four were women.

- Women hold just one in four executive leadership roles in ASX-300 companies.
- Women are more likely to feature in the executive leadership teams of ASX-100 companies, but almost half of ASX-100 companies still have no women in roles with profit and loss responsibilities.

Australia is not alone in this situation. Of the US Fortune 500 companies, only 8 per cent are led by women and less than 1 per cent led by women of colour. The under-representation of women in leadership positions worldwide is dire. The McKinsey *Women in the Workplace 2022* report backs the finding that women are being significantly underrepresented in leadership. Further, they found that companies are struggling to hold onto the relatively few women leaders they have – again, these dynamics are even more pronounced for women of colour.

What is even more alarming about these facts is when they are put in the context of research by Bain & Company, outlined in their *Everyday Moments of Truth* report, which identified that within the first two years of women entering the workforce, 43 per cent aspire to and have confidence in reaching a top management position, compared with 34 per cent of men. However, after two years, as both men and women gained experience, the research found that women's confidence and aspiration levels dropped to 16 per cent, compared with men at 34 per cent. This represents an alarming 60 per cent fall in women's confidence while men's confidence levels stayed the same.

The *Harvard Business Review* article 'How to close the gender gap' found that while companies do and are promoting their support of women's progression into leadership roles, what they fail to understand is the systemic barriers that are holding women back. They found gender bias and structural disadvantages are suppressing women's success at all stages, from recruitment through to retention.

The authors recommend that systematic changes be made across seven main areas of talent management:

- attracting candidates
- hiring employees
- integrating employees into organisations
- developing talent
- assessing performance and promotion
- managing compensation
- retaining good performers.

Thinking further about these recommendations and reflecting back on the personal stories and lived experiences that the amazing women we interviewed shared, it was interesting that we could align their PCMs to a corresponding area of talent management.

We are at such a crucial moment in corporate Australia and globally. Please use this context to understand that, in your personal PCM, potentially more is going on than what's happening directly to you. These contexts can help you shift your mindset to understanding your situation may be largely a systemic one, and one that is unlikely to be resolved until we have gender and diversity equity.

An appetite for change

COVID-19 created an appetite and a momentum for change in the workplace. It has proven that people can have flexible arrangements and most work can be done remotely. Marianne in her corporate career (and in pre-COVID times) was part of the Commonwealth Bank Australia's (CBA's) Gender Diversity Steering Committee, a committee that tried to make flexible work agreements for all work. However, suggested changes could never get traction across the business because many insisted there were technology or risk barriers. Sadly, it took a global pandemic to demonstrate that work and tasks could be achieved working remotely. Globally, the pandemic normalised flexible working arrangements and proved that almost any job could be done remotely. Having said that, we also want to acknowledge the extraordinary work from our frontline care workers who continue to work so hard, and acknowledge this does not apply to them. We aren't referring to this job family in this normalisation because, as expected, they still predominantly need to deal with people on an in-person basis. We're talking here about the corporate environment.

As we move into the 'new normal' following the pandemic, the temptation is to go back to the old ways. Designating only in-person working and traditional work days that don't fit in with modern lives is creeping back in. As proven over and over, this system suits men more than women. Women (and men) need advocacy to continue to support flexible arrangements to finally break down those structural barriers.

We hope that organisations will consider other factors and put more formal structures and policies in place, such as ensuring a reasonable number of meetings each day, having meeting-free days, and implementing realistic work capacity levels that don't push people into the kind of stress and anxiety that can lead to an erosion of confidence. These structures and policies are of critical importance to the topics that we've talked about in this book, such as psychological safety and a focus on health and wellbeing as a priority duty of care, and the opportunity for all employees to have support networks in place.

We are not suggesting that it's your sole responsibility to fix these systemic issues; we are suggesting that any women in leadership positions can be part of a collective effort to make an impact. During our research process in writing this book, and discussing the topics with our networks, both Marianne and Vanessa found it alarming that one of the only consistent issues that was shared by both men and women was the lack of support for women by women. No-one spoke about men not supporting each other. We found this devastating, especially because we both surround ourselves with so many amazing women lifting and supporting each other. We questioned why isn't this being noticed or seen, and now think it's because women do this more quietly than men. For system change, we need more women and even a greater number of men to continue to support women and each other, be advocates and be role models – and to do so 'loudly'. This will encourage other women and men to do the same and give more women opportunities.

It's time to talk about some of the steps or actions that you can take.

Playing a part in change

Marianne attended the 2022 annual Women in Super Christmas lunch, in Sydney, where one of the best stories was from Alexis George, the CEO of ASX-listed business AMP Limited. Alexis shared that after taking on the CEO role, she'd had a look through the organisation and found a female leader she thought had the potential to be a future CEO. Alexis invited her to have lunch. The leader was nervous about this invitation; however, Alexis shared that based on her observations of the leader's work performance and potential, Alexis decided that she was going to be her mentor, like it or not. You can imagine the confidence-boosting impact this had on that individual!

We've already talked about women's confidence in those early stages of a PCM, and how they may not want to ask or reach out for this type of support. Choosing, as a senior woman, to reach out and find other woman to mentor is a fantastic step forward. Your knowledge and experience, wisdom and comradeship will bring great value to others. You could also introduce women in your network to your male colleagues. This will help broaden their network – so next time a career opportunity comes up, that male colleague will have a diverse gender group to consider. Vanessa coaches many male executives who don't know where to start to broaden their networks. Let's help them. This is a great opportunity for us.

Another way to play a part in this change is to get involved in your workplace policy settings. Most corporates have working groups or gender steering committees, or diversity and inclusion councils. Make sure that your organisation has women represented in these groups. Ensure women have a voice to encourage and advocate, to keep or to develop important policy settings that are critical for women to flourish. You can use your influence and encouragement to ensure women utilise policies such as flexible working arrangements, childcare and carer's leave. Another great suggestion is to advocate these policies be gender neutral so all can use the provisions that encourage equality, such as flexible work and parental and general carer's leave.

Encourage men to join the groups that support women and promote the need to turn these inequality factors around. The Champions of Change Coalition (championsofchangecoalition.org/), for example, is a fantastic way for senior men to get involved. Focus groups exist across most industry sectors and are great networks. These focus groups often have networking opportunity lunches, so grab a table – and don't just take your group of female colleagues and friends. Instead, invite male colleagues in your organisation to come along. This can not only help them broaden their perspective and understanding of what it's like to be a minority in the group but also, importantly, encourage them to see talent around them and start to see what they may not have seen before – senior women in incredible roles.

Another great example of this role modelling is from Bernadette, who we introduced in chapter 5. Bernadette demonstrated that if change is to happen, the leader of the organisation needs to be an early adopter. She introduced flexible working and role-modelled how a four-day work week can be successful. Bernadette is a passionate advocate and recently appointed as Chair of the Family Friendly Workplaces Advisory Group. Bernadette uses every available opportunity to 'actively create an equal future, one conversation at a time'.

Finally, join some advocacy groups. So many industry and not-for-profit organisations have groups focused on making these changes happen. Some that we are involved in include:

- Australian Women in Resources Alliance (areea.com.au)
- Chief Executive Women (cew.org.au)
- Compliance and Risk Executive Women (crew-australia.com)
- Future Women (futurewomen.com)
- Franklin Women (franklinwomen.com.au)
- National Association of Women in Operations (nawo.org.au)
- National Committee for Women in Engineering (engineersaustralia.org.au)
- National Association of Women in Construction (nawic.com.au)
- The Inclusion Circle (formerly NEEOPA) (theinclusioncircle.org.au)
- Women on Boards (womenonboards.net)
- Women in Banking and Finance (wibf.org.au)
- Women in Data Science (widssydney.com.au)
- Women in Finance (womeninfinance.com.au)
- Women Leaders by the Circle (buscircle.com)
- Women Leaders in Sport (ausport.gov.au)
- Women in Media (womeninmedia.com.au)
- Women in Mining Network (ausimm.com)
- Women in Payments (womeninpayments.org)
- Women in Super (womeninsuper.com.au)
- Women in Technology (wit.org.au).

Every industry has such a group, so find the support group for your industry – and beyond. Some women feel embarrassed that we have all these networks and support groups. We would love to see the day when these groups become redundant. However, looking at the facts and figures outlined in this chapter, we are a long way from that yet. We need these groups to be advocating, supporting and vocal in policy setting, ensuring that we can shift this for the next generation.

Summing up

Many systems in society and the corporate environment still work against women and minority groups doing and being their best. This macro factor contributes – along with all the other factors covered in this book – to you feeling the way that you do during a PCM. Keep focused on yourself and what you can change, and move past the PCM. The more that women move through their PCM with strong support, the more choices they have to remain in top executive roles and take on more senior roles. In time, this will help turn the statistics around.

Change your mindset around the PCM and focus on what you can control. Think beyond the PCM. Work through the Think Beyond model to focus on yourself first to reach a state of calm and readiness. You will be able to gain clarity around what is possible for you, and then create your goals and your strategy for action. Set yourself up with the support and resources you need to commit to your success.

In a recent session with a number of senior women, including independent member for Warringah and former Australian Winter Olympian Zali Steggall, Christine Holgate – CEO of Toll Holdings, formerly CEO of Australia Post – had this powerful message:

> I was honoured and delighted to join Zali and the incredible panel
> of women for this important conversation. While we know there is
> more to be done, I am inspired that we are beginning to see women

of all ages and backgrounds speaking up, standing together and supporting one another towards this vital change. It is encouraging to have more and more men who are listening and speaking out in support of women for the inequality in society. We have a long way to go, but if we can strive to a culture where women have equal opportunity to thrive, we will thrive as a nation.

Well said, Christine Holgate!

Even ChatGPT sees the need for change

At the time of writing this book the debate over the use of AI tools such as ChatGPT emerged. Our book is based on our research, and we have shared this research and statistics throughout. We have also shared the strategies of experts on this topic, and drawn on our own experiences. So we now thought we would ask ChatGPT how we can improve the gender imbalance in leadership roles. ChatGPT tell us:

Getting more women in leadership roles requires a multifaceted approach that involves addressing systemic barriers, changing cultural attitudes and practices, and providing support and opportunities for women. Here are some ways to achieve this goal:

- **Promote gender diversity:** Organisations can promote gender diversity by setting diversity targets, publicly reporting on their progress, and holding leaders accountable for achieving these targets.
- **Challenge gender stereotypes:** Addressing gender stereotypes requires ongoing education and awareness-raising efforts. Organisations can promote gender-neutral language, offer training on unconscious bias, and encourage diversity in hiring practices.
- **Provide mentorship and sponsorship:** Providing mentorship and sponsorship opportunities for women

can help them develop the skills and networks necessary to advance to leadership roles. Leaders can actively seek out opportunities to mentor and sponsor women, and organisations can establish formal mentorship and sponsorship programs.

- **Create flexible work arrangements:** Flexible work arrangements, such as part-time or remote work options, can help women balance work and family responsibilities, allowing them to take on more significant leadership roles. Organisations can offer flexible work arrangements and promote a culture of work–life balance.

- **Address pay inequity:** Addressing pay inequity is crucial for promoting gender equality in leadership. Organisations can conduct regular pay audits, offer transparent salary structures, and ensure that women receive equal pay for equal work.

- **Provide leadership development opportunities:** Organisations can provide leadership development opportunities for women, such as training programs and leadership coaching, to help them develop the skills necessary to advance to leadership roles.

- **Celebrate and showcase female leaders:** Celebrating and showcasing female leaders can help to challenge gender stereotypes and promote diversity in leadership. Organisations can recognise and highlight the achievements of women in leadership roles, and promote them as role models for the next generation of female leaders.

Overall, getting more women in leadership roles requires a sustained and coordinated effort from leaders, organisations and individuals at all levels. By addressing systemic barriers, promoting cultural change, and providing support and opportunities for women, we can work towards a more gender-equal future.

Well said, ChatGPT! We can all do this together.

Conclusion

This is a book about your confidence journey. It is about the moment in your career when circumstances create a pivotal career moment (PCM), and how this can derail your confidence. Importantly, this book is about how you navigate through that PCM and recover. When something as significant as a PCM happens in your life, you often feel uneasy and unsure about what to do next. This book is all about helping you feel okay again. Life can be crappy. You can't control some of it. Don't be down on yourself – there are ways to get over it and back to your full potential. You have had a great career and then a bad moment happens. Don't personalise it. Understand it.

This book helps you navigate through your PCM to continue your successful career. We've shared our research with you and the stories of other successful female executives to reassure you that you are not alone. This way, when you reflect back on your PCM, you can see that at the time the situation and experience were stressful, but they made you think about what you want and helped you get on the path to what you value and what is important.

Imagine you have trust in yourself, your strengths and your abilities. You feel comfortable in who you are and your humanness. Imagine that you are confident. You are thriving in your career and your health and wellbeing are on track. You are surrounded and supported by your crew. You are the best version of yourself – happier, more content and appreciating your life. The stress you felt is gone or at a level you can manage. You hear only positive, constructive, supportive voices around you – including your inner voice – encouraging you on your journey ahead. This is all possible if you follow the steps outlined in this book.

Recognise that you are in a PCM and you need to stop the lack of confidence snowball. Then use the Think Beyond model to navigate your way through. Once you reach calm, clarity will come. That is the point when you can work with your crew to create your new future and commit to the right actions. Some of the biggest mistakes you can make are thinking confidence is an exterior behaviour and comparing yourself to others. This often leads to jumping into full action mode, making decisions before you are ready, setting off further confidence snowballs that lead to a career avalanche.

It's our goal to create a world where women bounce back from their PCM, stronger and with a positive focus on the future. This book gives you everything you need to do so. However, if you want personalised help, then it's an executive coach that you need.

We not only hope executive women feel more confident in themselves to navigate PCMs and to build a better and brighter future for themselves, but also hope they inspire other women on the journey. As one of our interviewees, Sally, said, 'You always had it in you. You just didn't know it.' It was always there – you had everything you needed from the start – but it's a journey.

Paulo Coelho's book *The Alchemist*, when read at a certain time of your life, changes your view on life because it's about taking that journey to find your own treasure. The protagonist finds it back where he started, but he never would have found it without the journey. It's the same for you. You've got everything you need; reflection unlocks the wisdom that comes from experience and the confidence that you can find it. The journey will not always be easy. Trust yourself. Enjoy it. The journey is the destination!

'What I'd say to my younger self': Final words from our interviewees

As the final question in our interviews, we asked our interviewees for the advice they'd give to their younger self, knowing what they do now. Here are their responses.

Anna

Currently a CEO in the for-purpose sector with prior CEO experience in a top ASX-200 company and board director.

'Identify lots of role models, women who appear confident, competent, accomplished, interesting, fabulous and confident in their intelligence to be successful. You can have any career, be anybody you want to be if you are educated and put your mind to it; have the confidence to give it a go. Then you realise, oh, actually, that wasn't so hard. Push boundaries and test yourself and then you will gain more confidence. It's not [about taking] a great leap from no confidence to full confidence; it is steps along the way.

Build resilience through trying something, knowing that you may not succeed. Assess the situation to understand what's the worst thing that could happen and just deal with it. Understand the real repercussions to failure – it's probably not as bad as you initially think. Seek mentors, both men and women.

Leave your ego at the door, and have the confidence to say what you think because your crazy idea may spark someone else's idea. Say something and ask questions. You will realise other people had the same question that you had.'

Amelia

A former CEO, and now non-executive director and chair for several ASX-listed organisations.

'I'd tell my younger self that perfection isn't about doing everything perfectly; it's about the desire to want to do it perfectly. It's about wanting to do things perfectly but it's not about being able do them all perfectly.

Just keep imagining that the impossible is possible. You never know what you really can do. It's not about winning an Olympic medal; it's about doing something you never thought you could. It's worth sticking to something. Whatever it is – it might be cooking a soufflé. You don't think you can cook [but] if you can read, you can cook. There are small steps you can take. It's like innovation – it's not just one big thing, it's a series of small steps put together consistently to be able to build on getting where you want. If you are here and want to be there, then what are the steps that you need to take to get there? If I'm a NED [non-executive director] but I want to be a chairperson, what are the gaps I need to close? Then you do those steps as best you can.

Having mentors is important. I've still got a mentor. He's the most delightful man. I've had a lot of mentors along the way. Sometimes you've got to accept the workplace scenario and be brave enough to step away. You can be stuck in that same environment and think it's unfair, or you can step away and make the change. You've nearly always got the power to make the change, so have the confidence or seek someone to help you to navigate the change.'

Audrey

An actuary, author and non-executive director in the superannuation and wealth management industry.

'To understand that you feel less confident, but you are able and capable.

Try to understand why you are less confident, to understand all the factors like hormones, like the way your brain works, how you are conditioned. If you can understand why and educate yourself to this, when you feel a lack of confidence you can anchor back to this knowledge through your experiences. If you don't have this broader understanding or an anchor, you may feel that you're the only one going through this.

Be determined. Confidence is a paradox; you might feel like you lack confidence, but this feeling can fuel an underlying determination and that is quite powerful, which can fuel your confidence. Be optimistic. It's not immediately obvious but it's there.'

Bernadette

An entrepreneur and business owner, growing a business that was acquired by a global leader in the people solutions space.

'Just opt into every opportunity that will allow you to stretch and to grow and to learn and to take a risk. Don't talk yourself down; it pretty much always works out. There's always something to take away and learn. Dismantle any walls or barriers that you're perceiving; just dismantle them quickly, and jump in.

Surround yourself with your cheer squad. Make sure that you've got a few key people, you know, who's on your board – who can you go to? I don't buy into the one mentor can be all things to all people. I think that you go to certain people for life coaching, others for financial commercial acumen, and others for creativity and marketing prowess. Have a few subject matter experts who you trust, who have deep smarts and expertise, and who you can pick up the phone to when you need it. But also find ways of giving back to them as well.

There are two streams: one is authenticity – what you believe in, being able to stand by that and not pretending to be something else – and the second is saying I don't know something, and I'll go and find out and get back to you.'

Catherine

An executive of large and complex government organisations, leading a range of functions, from customer strategy, corporate services and company secretary, to people and culture.

'I would just say to myself, it will be okay. You aren't meant to know everything there is to know to attempt something new. Don't put yourself under so much pressure. You're good enough and that is enough. You are not the tasks, the assignment, or the work. You are you! And you are tapping into your strengths. Remember to take care of yourself and have balance. It's hard to be confident if you're not eating well, not exercising and not sleeping enough. You can have it all, but you can't have it all at once.

You will meet lots of people who will believe in you – embrace their help. Your greatest learnings and growth will come from the toughest times. Remember to stay connected with loved ones and have fun.

I did at times put myself under a lot of pressure, I did not stay connected to what was important or have a balanced pace. And sometimes I did forget to have fun, because I was too busy feeling like an imposter or feeling like I'm not good enough. You still must be excellent at what you do, but that's different to wasted energy pushing yourself because you think you're not good enough. Redeposit that energy into the learning piece and the growing piece versus the worrying piece.'

Eliza

A senior people and culture executive with over 25 years' experience, across a range of industries, including financial services, professional services, IT, and the resources sector.

'You do you; don't try to be something you are not. Don't assume others know more than you do because they are in a more senior position. It's okay to not know everything. You can't fast track through life. You must live it to appreciate it – it's accumulative and compounding. You can't segment life like that.'

Emma

An executive in the media industry, and a journalist, presenter and author.

'You've got to back yourself. Find yourself some blokes to be in your tribe who are going to give you a different perspective. And while women tend to be supportive and will help you, we don't always see things the same as men. A different perspective is important. If we're in a man's world, we've got to get that side of things. Don't be afraid to fail because you do recover, and you come up with a different script the next time if there's an actual problem. And, you know, no-one is going to die through it, we're not surgeons. You've got to be a bit realistic about what is the worst thing that can happen. I think you still need the qualifications, and you need to have that level of professionalism. There's no point in having false confidence because we all judge people on that as well.

When I went to uni in the first place, I was always more interested in the arts, but I didn't back myself to think I could get a good job in that. I went into economics so that I'd get a good background, I could get a job in that area, it was well paid. Whereas I should've just backed myself and realised, "You can write. Oh look, you can be a comedy writer", but I didn't know those jobs existed. But if I got to pick something that I would really love, it would have been something a bit more creative. But I think, [I didn't have] the confidence to think that I could compete on those sorts of levels.

So, believe in yourself that you can compete at those levels. Find out what is available and have the confidence to push through to have a go. I had a fallback career, but I just did it because I didn't have the guts to go out and do something that I was actually passionate about. So, explore the possibilities to carry forward with your passion.'

Grace

A former senior executive career in the wealth management industry who has worked for large listed companies. She is now founder and CEO of a start-up technology company.

'Have that confidence to speak up; learn to own your own voice. Learn to trust that emotion that comes up when you are not so sure about something. Learn to trust this as it's usually a very good indicator that something is wrong. Rather than waiting to have all the pieces, put your hand up, trust your gut and say, "This feels wrong, explain it to me a bit more". Just trust your gut and keep asking questions because you're usually right.'

Kiara

A C-suite level executive with a passion for digital, media and tech-oriented businesses, and a group chief financial officer of an ASX-listed company.

'You've got all these great attributes of an entrepreneur, just pack up and go to the US, Silicon Valley, or set up your own business and see how it goes. Use all the elements – passion, creativity, being driven, a finance background – and run your own business. I still decided that staying in corporate was what I wanted to do.

Take even more risks because it doesn't matter when you're young. You've got a 25-year window ahead of you still in terms of corporate life, so if something went wrong, you'll still have your 30s, 40s and 50s to recover from a corporate perspective. You have fewer financial commitments, and less personal commitments in your 20s – so if you want to make anything of your life, test it, then do it now!

Sally

An entrepreneur, business owner and author, with 30 years' experience across the financial services and media industries.

'You always had it in you. You just didn't know it. It's gonna be alright. It was always there; you had everything you needed from the start, but it's a journey.'

Susan

A strategic senior technology executive, who has managed large scale IT operations across an international footprint and led complex digital transformation project portfolios within fast moving consumer goods (FMCG), retail, financial services and management consulting industries.

'Trust in your ability. Ask yourself what's the worst thing that could happen? Surround yourself with good people. Also, go with your gut – sometimes if it doesn't feel right, then it's not right for you. Embrace self-worth and self-care; looking after yourself is important. Take people along with you and help others on that journey and try to focus on giving back. Most people are in the same boat, and they're struggling with the same things. It's not all about you – how can you help other people on the journey? Building confidence in others can be a self-fulfilling thing as well.'

Victoria

A chief operating officer with deep experience in leading transformation through mergers and acquisitions in the financial services sector.

'Speak up sooner, you have a voice; it might be different to everyone else around the table, but just speak up. Be brave – by speaking up you may help someone else who hasn't yet found their voice. The other point is to give it a go. Don't just think about it; get in there, boots and all.

Be humble; the minute you think you are better than anyone else in the room is the day you may need to step away from the tools. Humility and kindness. Be kind to others but also be kind to yourself. Recognise you know when to speak out, and that your differences compared with others is what makes you unique. Work hard at doing the right thing.'

Yasmin

A CEO of a high-profile Australian industry body with a career in senior corporate and regulatory affairs, media, government relations and C-suite roles in the media and entertainment sector, as well as non-executive and advisory roles.

'You're going to be fine! Keep doing what you're doing. I think if somebody said that to me, when I was young – "You're going to be fine, keep doing what you're doing" – that would have been helpful. It sounds simple. Lived experience will build your confidence and you will realise this when you come out the other side and come to terms with what happened. Reframe challenging times for yourself. Just hang in there.

I think younger women can be intimidated by older successful women. But in my experience, there are a lot of older successful women who love to help, give encouragement, or open a door for you. So don't be afraid to approach people and make a connection.'

About the authors

Vanessa Venning

Vanessa is a leading executive coach, facilitator and presenter and has worked with hundreds of senior leaders across global businesses. She helps executives to think beyond to navigate personal and professional change, rediscover career confidence and design transition strategies for future executive, Non-Executive Board and Portfolio careers.

Vanessa draws on wisdom gained from a diverse and unique career. She was a registered nurse, a professional singer and recording artist, creating history recording the first multi-track digital single in Australia and entered in the National Film and Sound Archives, and a television presenter with Seven Network. Vanessa transitioned to a successful corporate career as a People and Culture Executive spanning diverse sectors including technology, media, professional services, travel, retail and medical devices.

Vanessa holds a Bachelor and Master of Business| University of Technology Sydney. She is a Graduate of the Australian Institute of Company Directors; Brain-Based Coaching Certification | Neuroleadership Institute; Foundations of Applied Neuroscience Certification | Neuroscience Academy; Accredited Whole Brain Thinking practitioner. She is a member of the ICF (International Coaching Federation).

Marianne Perkovic

Marianne's career spans three decades of experience across Executive, Board Director and Trustee roles in Banking and Financial Services, Financial Advice, Superannuation, and Fashion. Her journey as a contemporary leader and strategic thinker has been characterised by her ability to work in complex and challenging environments. She has held senior roles at large corporations such as the Commonwealth Bank of Australia and KPMG Australia. Marianne has led large (over 2,000 people), diverse teams, inspiring them to lead with authenticity and confidence. In 2006 she was reported as the youngest female CEO of an ASX-listed company. In 2017 she received the Financial Services Council Industry award for her work in the financial services sector.

Marianne holds a Bachelor of Economics with a Business Law major from Macquarie University and a Master of Business Administration from the Macquarie Graduate School of Management. She is a Graduate of the Australian Institute of Company Directors, a member of Chief Executive Women and Chair of the Australian Fashion Council.

Marianne is an advocate for diversity and inclusion and driving sustainable transformation with a positive environmental and social impact.

devlinnoble.com.au